FROM SPECIAL ED. TO SPELMAN:
Against All Odds

Tanell Vashawn Allen, MDiv

FROM SPECIAL ED TO SPELMAN: AGAINST ALL ODDS: By Tanell Vashawn Allen, M Div

Copyright © 2022 by Tanell Vashawn Allen

All rights reserved. No part of this book may be reproduced or transmitted in any form or by any means without written permission from the author.

ISBN (XXXXXXXXXXXXX)

Library of Congress Control Number

Published in Brooklyn, New York, By Tanell Vashawn Allen. Scripture quotations noted in KJV are from the King James version. Copywritten 1979, 1980, 1982, by Thomas Nelson, Incorporated Publishers used by permission all rights reserved.

Some of the names and locations in this book have been changed to protect the identities of the individuals I am writing about in this book.

Thank you for supporting the vision!

Front cover photo by: Takia Ebonee Lambert. https://calendly.com/tk-consulting-design/initial-consultation

Hair by: Color Me Mocha Glam Squad

MUA Tanell Vashashawn Allen

Book cover design https://www/fiverr.com/germancreative

Edited by: Jeannine email: blueclematis77@gmail.com

Printed in USA by Mocha In My Coffee: Phone: (352) 807-4564 Email: tanellallen@gmail.com On-Line Chat: go to our website, www.mochainmycoffee.square.site.com

Dedication

This book is dedicated to two extraordinary women in my life. The first is my beautiful, loving, intelligent, and supportive sister Nada Allen. I am who I am because of you and all that you do. Thank you for teaching me how to be *greatness in motion.* People may come and go, but you are the one person who God uses to keep me grounded, and humble. Always taking time to inspire me, to try new things, fulfill my purpose, and live out my dreams.

Your words always ring in my spirit when I pursue new endeavors, goals, and dreams that challenge me.

"Don't ever let anyone tell you what you can or cannot do! You hear me? I don't care if you have to knock the door down. Don't you let nothing, or nobody get in the way of your dreams."

There are so many things that you have taught me over the years. Like how to save, scout out my next home, run my business, and cut off dead-end relationships and friendships. Yet, most of all you taught me how to forgive.

Thank you for always taking the time to show me what love really looks and feels like. I am honored that God handpicked us to be sisters and best friends.

It would be selfish of me to pretend that you are only supportive of me, but the truth is you share and spread that same motivation and inspiration everywhere you go, and with everyone you meet. Thank you for being *my best friend and [s]hero.*

Secondly, this book is dedicated to the loving memory of Rev. Dr. Barbara Mitchell. She was affectionately known as Ms. Barbara, or "Momma Boom-Boom." Always taking time to share pearls of wisdom with us "Young Phillies!" She was an excellent student of knowledge, a scholar, a mentor, an educator, a reverend, a friend, a sister, and a motherly figure. She reminded everyone who ever met her of the song, "Grandma's Hands."

She made the best carrot cake this side of heaven. She introduced many of us to some of the finer things in life, such as eating alligators and fried frog legs and learning about different cultures around the world.

Ms. Barbara encouraged many of us to embrace change and to use our personal experiences to push us out of our comfort zones and fuel our purpose.

Her love and her quest for learning have inspired many of her peers to pursue their dreams and live out their calling. Ms. Barbara had a presence about her when she entered a room or opened her mouth. You recognized the greatness of the shoulders she stood on as she passed the torch to other Womanist and Black Theologians. She never allowed us to forget why we cannot afford to drop the ball, and that people were waiting for us to change the world, one sermon at a time.

Rev. Dr. Barbara Mitchell may be gone, but she will never be forgotten. We will forever be thankful for her touching our lives with her legacy of greatness! Rest in Heaven, my friend, my sister, and my colleague.

Acknowledgments

It is not who as much as it is what. What they have taught me individually and collectively is remarkable. They were everything I desperately needed them to be, without asking. Many of them took on the daunting task of educating, reaching, mentoring, counseling, and seeing, but most of all inspiring me. They did so by seeing something in me while I navigated some of the roughest drafts of my life.

They believed that my life could have a plot change and that it had the potential to be a bestseller. They say, "Those who can't do, teach." I am glad that most of the people who have had the most significant impact on me were underestimated by this simple cliché. Maybe this is why some of them were able to recognize the greatness that lay locked away inside of me. I would like to acknowledge every teacher and professor who never gave up on me and took the time to invest in educating, motivating, counseling, tutoring, mentoring, and inspiring me to be a "world changer."

Foreword

In my fifty years as an educator, I witnessed how debilitating the school experience can be for students who see themselves as academically deficient in the classroom and unwelcome in the school. I saw how being labeled disabled, disordered, or deficient impacted the well-being of students in ways that negatively stayed with them throughout their lives, always casting a shadow over their intelligence.

When I first met Tanell, she was in the eighth grade, and I was a doctoral student assigned to her school as part of a parent involvement grant. After twenty years of being a special educator, I was returning to the university to take a critical look at the medical model dominating special education, speaking with such certainty that lack of academic progress stems from a disability within the student rather than the curriculum limitations placed on them by our educational practices.

Tanell was said to have a learning disability. She was pulled from her classroom daily to receive special services that focused on remediating her below-grade-level performance on standardized tests. The work assigned often mimicked state assessment exams so students, like Tanell, would be familiar with the format.

Goals and objectives included classroom behavior that focused on completion of assignments and, in Tanell's case, her attitude, which referred to the rolling of her eyes and ignoring who was speaking to her when she felt she was being unjustly reprimanded and singled out.

One day, Tanell invited me to her church to hear her speak. When she stood at the pulpit I was transformed by her poise, confidence, passion, clarity, and ability to capture our attention and stimulate us to think. I could see that Tanell was a gifted storyteller, a dramatic orator, and a deep thinker, who trusted her own worth and had something important to say.

At school, in a discussion about Tanell's behavior I shared my experience and impressions from her church presentation. The response was: if only she would behave that way at school. But school did not offer Tanell the venue for learning that embraced the strengths, skills, abilities, and gifts brewing inside her. I could see Tanell was bursting at the seams with ideas and talents that were being suppressed by school policies.

It was painful to watch Tanell struggle, trying to learn in a setting that was restrictive, with a curriculum focused on remediation.

I could see this was not a natural way for Tanell to learn, to make meaning and gain understanding, to foster her sense of inquiry, to tap into her creative mind, her passion, her curious nature, her bright intellect. Over the years I have seen the mark left on students like Tanell as they transition to adulthood, measuring themselves against others and feeling inadequate, less confident, and unsure of themselves. I often imagine a different middle school experience for Tanell where she is flourishing in theater or working on a school performance, where she is a respected member of the debate team because of her genuineness and passion, and where she is running for class president because she has strong leadership skills, and her peers look up to her. But that wasn't her experience.

It wasn't ours either. We missed out on an opportunity to provide Tanell with an academic experience that nurtured, challenged, and supported her ways of knowing.

In this inspirational memoir, Tanell shows us the incredible hold being labeled learning disabled has had on her life. How she accepted it as a truth about her intellect and her capacity to learn. How she carried it as a burden throughout her academic experience. While painful to read it is also uplifting because we see Tanell extricate herself from the cloak of disability, as something that was put upon her, not something that is inherent in her.

Her book is intended to inspire others to see themselves in all their magnificence and invite them to step away from the label that has othered them. I am honored to have the privilege of writing this foreword for Tanell's book. Her message is not only vital for people who have had a similar experience and are looking for inspiration, but it is also essential to for educators to recognize the importance of creating an inviting, engaging, stimulating academic experience for all learners in the classroom.

Sincerely,

Susan Perez, Ph.D. Retired School Principal

Foreword

Tanell V. Allen, what an honor and privilege it is to watch you grow, dare to dream, and accomplish your goals against all the odds that have been dealt to you. To see how you used to stand up in the mirror as a little girl for hours, primping around, and speaking over your life, was something I had never seen before.

As a little girl, you dared to speak over yourself through positive affirmations. You believed in yourself when others doubted you. You overcame being told what you wouldn't or couldn't do. Despite your difficulties with learning, you refused to give up. Your strong faith in God and your relentless quest to earn an education turned your dreams into visions, and visions into reality.

You have always refused to take *no* as the final answer without knowing *why*. You once asked me, "Can I paint my room purple and black?"

I said, "No!"

You replied, "I do not know why not! You said it was my room. I should be able to paint it any color I want. If it is my room."

You have always been a free thinker and one who refused to allow others to tell you who you were, what you could do, or stifle your creativity.

I remember when the teachers labeled you as having a learning disability you refused to accept that label.

You said, with tears in your eyes, "Grandma, they say, 'I am slow, and that I won't graduate, and if so, it will take five years.' Grandma, I am not slow. I am smart and I can do this. I can learn in the regular classes like everyone else. ***I AM GOING TO GRADUATE AT THE TOP OF MY CLASS.***"

Having watched you struggle and endure from a young age until now has inspired and challenged me to see people based on their character and potential. Not just who they are and not what they appear to be.

Now seeing the results of a little girl who dared to dream big and spoke over herself, now transformed into a well-balanced, educated, young lady with a master's degree and pursuing a PhD amazes me. You have accomplished so much and have traveled and lived in China, Germany, Chicago, Atlanta, Dade City, Trinidad, Saint Martin, and New York, the sky is not the limit for you.

I know that God is fulfilling all of those big dreams you have. To see this book come to fruition has been a dream of yours for many years. I know it is coming straight from your heart and it will be as inspiring as the first one. In this book your faith, creativity, wisdom, and passion will encourage millions to "take the labels off" and "cultivate the greatness inside of them."

You have proven time and time again with God on your side never to underestimate you.

God is ordering your steps; continue to allow God to work through you. Continue to follow your dreams, grow, and believe that "with God all things are possible. God is a rewarder of those who seek him."

I have never been prouder of you, my dear Granddaughter.

Elder Pastor Fannie Gentles

Introduction

For me, learning has always been a struggle. I used to cry and have emotional tantrums due to this challenge. I did not understand why God created me this way. Why did I have to fight so hard to learn what came so easily to others? I remember sitting in class with tears running down my face because no matter how hard I tried, I could not keep up, or understand what I was being taught.

Some of my peers played, talked, and misbehaved in class and still were able to run circles around me academically. I silently prayed as clouds of frustration and irritation hovered over me, that God would make me smart like everybody else. At 41 years old I still felt myself praying this same simple childlike prayer.

I thought that the more degrees I earned, the smarter I would be. The truth is that I did become smarter, but it did not make learning easier for me. However, I did learn how to become a professional student—how to use the resources that were available to assist me. I also discovered what learning style worked for me.

Yet I still wrestled with feelings of low self-efficacy. The degrees never took away those insecurities that I had harbored for so many years.

Some labels can have ways of defining and restricting people from tapping into the greatness within them.

For years, I allowed the labels that the education system placed on me to stop me from believing that I was intelligent or competent. I learned to always doubt and second-guess myself, but something about my faith in God always allowed me to dream big despite my insecurities.

I've learned that if I have faith and take with me the three D's of success—dedication, discipline, and determination—I am unstoppable at achieving any goal I set for myself. I've also realized that I do not have to be the sharpest tool in the shed, but I have to use the tools and resources in my hand to have a fighting chance at mastering what others more easily achieve.

Having a learning disability is nothing to be ashamed of. It does not mean you are not capable of learning. You have to consider that your learning style may be different, but it is not useless. Tell yourself, *"I am a creative and intellectual genius."*

One's attitude and way of thinking go a long way when you are fighting against the odds that have been dealt to you. Your perspective is everything. What you choose to believe and the choices you make determine if you will live out your purpose or wake up every day with a Pop-Tart perspective of life. Pop-tarts do not take any planning, they are not healthy, and offer limited nutritional value.

They are sweet, convenient, and a meal filler. You don't want to settle for having unhealthy, convenient, and counterfeit encounters in life.

You were not created to settle for living a convenient life, regurgitating information, or simply just existing. Nor were you created to just go through the motions of life, like you are not living life to the fullest. I am not talking about "riding on alligators" and jumping out of planes.

I am talking about never truly knowing your purpose, not learning to serve humanity with empathy and compassion, not cultivating the best version of yourself, not touching the face of God, or embracing the presence and peace of God.

When we can do these things, we can honestly say we are living our lives full-on and the lessons we are learning along the journey are our best teachers.

Ask yourself this powerful question: "What is my perspective on life and learning?"

Table of Contents

Dedication III

Acknowledgments V

Foreword VI

Foreword IX

Introduction XI

Chapter 1: I Am Not Stupid, Dumb, or Crazy 1

Chapter 2: Trading Touches for Help 5

Chapter 3: Taking the Labels Off 9

Chapter 4: My Baby Leaped 25

Chapter 5: Tearing Down My Rocky Foundation 30

Chapter 6: I Am a Dreamer 41

Chapter 7: Crying in the Closet 47

Chapter 8: I am Your Pusher 52

Chapter 9: The Hardest Thing 60

Chapter 10: My Math is Bad: Two Years = Four Years 66

Chapter 11: Kicking Down Doors 71

Chapter 12: Not Everyone is Going to be Happy for You 74

Chapter 13: "Can You Wear White, Young Lady?" 81

Chapter 14: Living My Dream 88

Chapter 15: History in the Making 105

Chapter 16: When Man Says No but God Says Yes! 109

Chapter 17: Faith Laced with Grief and Depression 114

Chapter 18: "Harpo, Who That Man Is" 119

Chapter 19: Laying on of Hands 131

Chapter 20: I Made It 138

Chapter 21: Daring to Dream Beyond Spelman Gates ... 142

Chapter 1

I Am Not Stupid, Dumb, or Crazy

> *I've learned that people will forget what you said, people will forget what you did, but people will never forget how you made them feel.*
>
> *-Dr. Maya Angelou*

Dear Oprah,

Hello, my name is Tanell Vashawn Allen. I always knew something was wrong with me when it came to learning. I have a documented learning disability. Some teachers took the extra time needed to teach me, while others were ok with me slipping through the cracks of the educational system.

I used to sit in class and cry because I did not know how to do the work and I lacked confidence in myself being able to do the work. Learning requires one to understand the material being taught, retain information, and be confident in one's ability to obtain the information.

Many children lack these and other basic skills because they may have difficulties learning due to undocumented learning and other disabilities, that prohibit them from focusing.

Perhaps they were not taught the necessary skills by their parents or may have experienced a traumatic childhood that did not foster learning, self-efficacy, or confidence.

Some children may have come from poor educational and socioeconomic backgrounds that did not provide a good education. There are others whose disabilities hinder them from learning at the same pace as others. Imagine having a learning disability, coupled with a poor educational system, and growing up in a troubled home. This could hinder even some of the brightest minds or alter their learning style.

Once I was diagnosed with learning and emotional disabilities, I spent most of my time trying to hide them from others. I spent many days denying the extra help I needed to be successful out of shame and the fear of being labeled as "other." I had to take time to learn what works best for me. In doing so, I have developed some tools and tips to help assist not only me but other students and working professionals with disabilities.

I am writing to inquire about being a part of your master class segment. It would be a great honor to share my story with you and to inspire and help others with learning and emotional disorders. I would like to share with your audience how I went From Special Ed to Spelman! I know you are no longer a talk show host, but the owner of Oprah Winfrey Network (OWN). It has been my dream to share my story with you for almost two decades; although it has been a long time, my dream has never faltered.

Oprah, being a part of your Master Life Classes would be a distinguished honor for me.

This great opportunity would allow me to reach a broader audience to share how they may be able to overcome the odds that were dealt to them, or more specifically, how they may be able to take the labels off that confine their untapped potential. I believe that sharing my journey through your media platform is a part of my purpose in life.

I never want another person to feel or think like I did. There were many times over the years that I sat in classes and wished I could have disappeared. I have lost count of how many times I have cried out to God in frustration with myself, asking God, Why? Why did you create me this way?"

Why am I so stupid? Why can't I do anything right? I was pleading with Him to give me wisdom and intellect, so I could be smart like the other kids in my class that somehow got it all the time. While I was sitting there trying to figure out how to get to the answer.

Even experts on disabilities cannot fully articulate how I really felt, or what was truly best for me. Only someone who has a disability can really understand how I felt. Experts may have some suggestions about what may work for you. Still, their suggestions come with risks because there are so many ways people learn that they may have not considered or studied yet.

The educational system does not foster true creativity. I have learned that I have a learning style that works for me, and so do so many others with disabilities. Dr. Susan Perez asserts, "I don't like the label disability. It makes students feel ashamed, stupid, and embarrassed. I never knew a student in special ed who was not embarrassed. The system makes the students feel they failed when the system failed them."

As I stated before, I would be honored to share my experience and perspective of a person being labeled as learning disabled and how I chose to take the label off, flip it, reject it, or make it work for me.

Sincerely,

Tanell Vashawn Allen

Pearls of Wisdom

I am Not Stupid, Dumb, or Crazy

- ➢ Know who you are and who you are not. Do not allow others to try to convince you of something that does not ring true to who you are at the core of your being.
- ➢ Do not allow others to insult your intelligence.
- ➢ Hold tight to your personal convictions, but be open to hearing others' perspectives.
- ➢ Keep a tribe of core people who will encourage you, support you, and tell you when you are right, but love you enough to tell you when you are wrong.
- ➢ Never be afraid to ask what others deem to be a stupid question.
- ➢ It is OK to get a second opinion. Opinions are not written in stone, and at the end of the day, an
- ➢ opinion is just that. You can take it or leave it.
- ➢ God created you, so He knows more about you than anyone else.
- ➢ God is the sole expert concerning all things you.
- ➢ Your perspectives and beliefs about yourself have more weight than anyone else's.

Chapter 2

Trading Touches for Help

> *Be careful who you allow to sow into you, because they [will think they] have the right to take from you.*
> —Apostle Tammy Willis

I had in School Suspension (ISS) for some dumb reason. I was not always the best-behaved kid in school. We were placed in this little room and not allowed to talk, leave, go to recess, or eat lunch with the rest of the class. In fact, someone had to bring us our lunch to eat in this little room. The people who came to check on us were not nice, not even a little. Thinking back, in some ways, it must have felt like being in a detention center or jail.

I was in there with this Latino boy who was at least five years older than me. Of course, he knew more about multiplication than I did. I could not figure out how to multiply those damn apples for the life of me. He offered to help me, but in exchange, I had to touch his private parts. To some degree, I knew what he was asking me to do was wrong.

I was old enough to know not to touch another person's private parts; they're called private parts because they're supposed to be kept private.

But I was a child so did not fully understand that I was being sexually abused by an older kid.

I was really desperate and just wanted help. I did not want to feel like a failure because I did not complete my assignments by the end of the day.

I had been sitting there crying, frustrated, most of the day. I tried, but I just could not do some of the work that my teacher had sent for me to complete... So, **I did it**. I was so afraid of getting caught, but I was more afraid of not having work finished and feeling like a failure. I think in my mind, I wanted to prove to my teacher I was smart, but I was not. In learning, confidence is a must, but I lacked it.

At first, I just tried to kind of touch him with the pencil, but that did not work. He said, "No, you have to touch *it* with your hand." I touched him as quickly as I could, then snatched my hand back as if I had just touched a hot stove. If he did not like the way I touched him, he would tell me I had to do it again before he would calculate the answer on his fingers and give it to me.

Looking back, I remember him not being bad-looking, he was kind of cute. Yet I also remember from that day forward not liking him as a person. Years later I saw him on the street, just the sight of him irritated me to the point I just wanted to smack the shit out of him. I reminded myself that this was what the old Tanell would do.

The old me was very emotional and impulsive. The new me is a woman in control.

I used to act and respond out of anger, not really thinking about the consequences until I became a Christian. I also am very intentional in debunking the myth of the *Angry Black Woman*.

I inhaled and exhaled deeply at the traumatic memory, knowing that the new Tanell was going to forgive him and herself for being young and foolish. However, I did call him a rat bastard before I repented and asked God to help embrace forgiveness.

Now that I'm an adult, I am more solution-oriented in finding out how I can get the answers I need to resolve past traumas, defuse conflicts, and complete projects.

I start projects early and ask for help if I need it. One of the most important lessons I have learned over the years is to give myself the grace to grow in my learning style, gifting, calling, forgiving, and anointing.

Pearls of Wisdom

Trading Touches for Help

- ➢ No one has the right to your body in exchange for helping you.
- ➢ Help should never come with strings attached to it, especially sexual strings.
- ➢ If someone asks you to touch them in an inappropriate way, never be afraid to let an adult or someone in authority know.
- ➢ Never allow fear to be your motivation.
- ➢ Never do things that you are personally uncomfortable with.
- ➢ Forgiveness is a must to embrace healing.

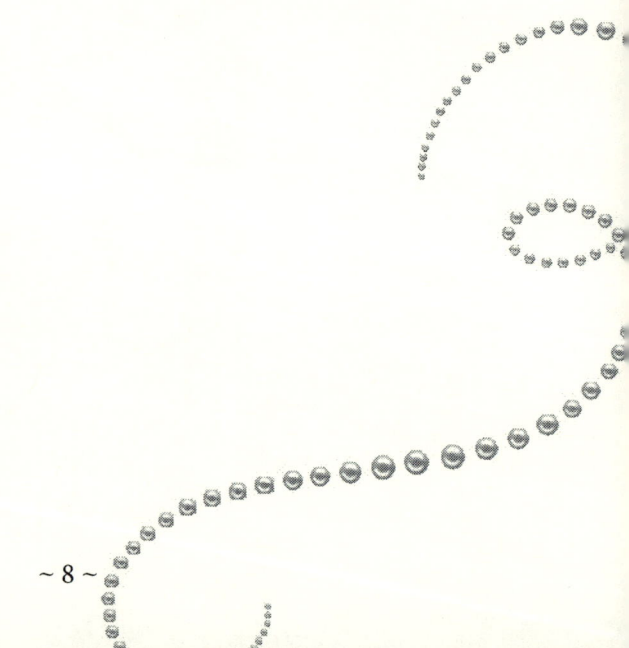

Chapter 3

Taking the Labels Off

> *Labels don't define you. No one else's name can make me feel sure of who I am. If I wear a brand name on the outside, but I don't know it on the inside, if my identity is given through a gift I have or even a label that people confer on me, I will always be a slave to their label.... Peel off the labels that have been applied to you. Only fathers have naming rights.*
>
> —Pastor Steven Furtick

All my life, many people have said that my learning disability would prevent me from excelling academically. When I was in the eighth grade, a group of educators told my grandmother, Foxy, and me that I would not graduate from high school and that if I did, it would take five years.

As my grandmother and I sat listening to my teachers, the school's speech therapist, and the school psychologist told us that I was not able to learn at the same pace as my peers, I was floored. Anger growing toward each of them, I was determined to prove the educators wrong. How dare they tell me to my face what I cannot do. I was always taught to never say never, nor to accept what others say I can or cannot do if it does not resonate with my spirit. This meeting was supposed to discuss my Individual Educational Plan (IEP), but it felt like they were sucking the very life out of my soul.

I knew it was meant to be a meeting to help me with my academic and emotional needs and goals, but it began to make me feel discouraged and hopeless.

I felt ambushed. As I listened, my heart began to beat violently and passionately in my chest, and I felt the blood coursing through my veins running hotter. I felt like the very people who should have been advocating for me were stifling my growth because they did not believe in me, know me, or even take the time to develop a plan to help me unlock my potential as a student. All they saw was that ***I was not their kind of smart***, meaning I did not learn or process things the way they felt I should. So, they forecasted a dark shadow over my academic future.

My face flushed, my ears were physically stinging as if someone had slapped my ears, every nerve in my body was on edge. I tried to fight what I was feeling inside by holding back the tears trying to escape from the windows of my soul. I felt like these people were killing the very spirit in me.

As they talked to my grandmother, she took in all of their words. I saw her look at me quickly. Her gaze went back to the experts as if she was still trying to make up her mind if she was going to believe what they were saying about me. She sat in silence and listened, slowly soaking up the information they were saying like a sponge.

I was hurt. I wanted her to say something in my defense. I'm not sure what she would have said at that moment, but *something* would have been better than the silence that was speaking volumes to me. It seemed at any moment I was going to lose it to the whole panel of experts. I wanted to jump out of my seat, flip the table, lose control of all of my emotions, turn green, and morph into She-Hulk. Later that week, I heard my grandmother sharing with my Auntie Meka what was said in the IEP meeting. "They said Nell has the mentality of a six-year-old and that she won't be able to graduate from high school."

I always felt S-L-O-W when it came to engaging with my Auntie Meka. My Auntie is more than smart, she is brilliant. I wish I was as smart as her. She graduated valedictorian, from both her grammar and high school. At the time, she was in college studying to become a teacher. Meka was the first of my aunties to go away to college. I loved it when she came home from college. She even talked as if she was super smart.

Growing up in the South in a small town like Dade City Florida, I was not privy to seeing or knowing many educated Black women personally even though there were many. One exception was my older cousin Jen on my father's side, who was an educator. I did not see many role models like her. Yet my Auntie Meka inspired me to want to go to college and excel academically. I wanted to be just like her in every way. I even learned how to speak like her and mimic her mannerisms.

Stubbornly and teary-eyed, I silently swore that I would graduate from high school and become somebody. *God no! These people think I am stupid, but I am smart."* I told myself, *I can do anything with God. If I set my mind to it, I can do it, I can graduate on time.*

I was right, I could do it. I graduated in four years, thirteenth in my class, with honors, just like I knew I could.

Ever since I was a child, I have stood up in front of the mirror, prophesying and speaking over my life. I don't think I really knew what I was doing back when I first started speaking over myself. I wanted to graduate as valedictorian of my high school class. But I quickly learned that it was easier said than done for most people, especially when you have a disability. Despite this, I refused to quit or to bow out gracefully at achieving my goal. It required a lot of hard work, sacrifice, and dedication. Some people felt I needed to just focus on graduating, but I would not settle for just graduating.

From the time I was in grade school, I had learned how to be grade-focused rather than learning-focused. As I matriculated through the educational system, I became obsessed with getting good grades.

The better my grades were, the smarter I felt. I wanted to be intelligent and hated not being able to spell some of the simplest words. I often tried to hide the fact that I had a learning disability because of the negative stigma associated with being "other" when it came to learning.

Somewhere within me, I started thinking that with every degree I earned, I would be able to remove the labels that the education system placed on me. I was in an eternal war within myself to prove I was smart enough and good enough to be deemed intelligent.

In my senior year of high school, I took the ACT and scored a ten out of a score of 36. By the time I finished reading one section, the others were moving on to the next section. When I received my test results back, all I could see was failure and defeat. I felt like someone had smacked me in my face. I could feel the pain of that slap on my face, the muscles in my chest tightening and my cheeks stinging. It felt like I was dying. I was suffocating from the threat of my dream of a higher education being denied. Unsure what to do, I was too embarrassed to share my defeat with my family.

Even though Meka and I lived under the same roof, I was too intimidated by my feelings of inferiority to ask her for help. She was an excellent math teacher, and I was failing math, yet I never liked asking her for help. On top of feeling dumb, I was secretly envious of her intellectual abilities. I'd rather flunk math with flying colors than ask her for help, which was silly, but at that moment I had to hold onto what strand of dignity I had.

Some people never fully understand how embarrassing it is for those who have learning disabilities. There were times I was shamed by my teachers and my peers and made fun of in my math and chemistry classes because I didn't know the answers to some of the questions when I was called upon. The last thing I wanted to happen was for me to bring all that trauma home with me. *I need my home life to be different*, I told myself. I don't believe my Auntie Meka would have ever done this to me, or any other student, but I never wanted to find out.

My Aunt's opinion of my intellectual abilities always meant a lot to me. My grandmother Foxy always beamed with such pride when she spoke of my aunts' and uncles' accomplishments. Just once, I wished I could have made my aunt and grandmother feel the same way about me. It wasn't until I was much older that I had the honor of learning how proud my grandmother was of me.

She stated during a heated discussion with my Aunt Meka, "That school ain't shit; my granddaughter graduated from Spelman College, you hear me."

On the inside, I beamed as I heard my grandma call me her granddaughter and acknowledge my accomplishment of graduating from Spelman College. I bet you are wondering how I accomplished this.

I had to face the reality that I was never going to make it in life hoping and wishing I did not have a learning disability or being ashamed of having a learning disability. Yet I used to live in fear of people finding out. I thought they would see me as being less intelligent, unemployable, or less successful.

I had allowed this label to lord over me and tell me what I could and could not do. Once I learned to take back all the power and authority I was giving it, I was able to flip the label and make it work for me. If I were to start a support group for people with learning disabilities, I would start things off by saying, "Hello, my name is Tanell Vashawn Allen and I have been labeled as having a learning disability. However, I choose not to allow any dis-ability to define who I am, as a person, my worth, my value, or my intellectual abilities.

I am a freaking creative genius. Each of us has strengths and weaknesses. Some people say, "You should focus on your strengths and not your weaknesses." I don't think this is a good habit.

Yes, focus on your strengths, but where would we be without our weaknesses? Our weaknesses illustrate our strengths and keep us humble.

They also teach us to strive to be better if we work on improving them instead of ignoring them.

If I had just given up because someone said, "She is not going to graduate and if she does, it is going to take five years," I would not have a Master of Divinity degree today. You have to choose to take the labels off by not accepting everything that others may say about you.

There is a scripture that asserts, "Life and death is in the power of the tongue," and there is so much truth in this. Regardless if the label is true or false, it is up to you to speak life to it by proving to all who said, "You can't or won't," wrong. I am *more* than capable of learning.

Based on the education system's standards of learning and how learning is "supposed" to happen, the label of learning disabled was accurate for me. Yet not accurate based on my individual style of learning. The question, then, becomes "What am I going to do about it?" Was I going to believe that I could not graduate? Was I going to allow what these experts, who didn't know me, said to stop me? Was I going to use my disability as an excuse to not excel academically, or was I going to prove everyone wrong? I was determined to come out swinging and fighting against the odds that had been dealt to me for my entire life.

When you choose to make the label work for you, you have no other choice but to put in the effort. For me, I have to become laser focused. I have to assess the pros and cons of the label that is trying to be applied to the fabric of my being. You can begin by decoding and researching these labels. This helps you to figure out your flipping strategy.

Often when labels are placed on us we go along with them and fail to ask vital questions to help us learn how to *flip the labels, according to our needs.*

Once you acknowledge that "I have a learning disability," you can ask," What are the resources available to help me succeed like any other student?" You say" My reading and math skills are not where they should be", so now ask, "What is the plan to assist me in improving them, or to get them on the right track?

What is this plan called? Whose job is it to assist me with achieving my academic and social goals? Who supervises those individuals?" How can we tell if the goals were met with satisfaction? How is this measured, and how often? These are all valid questions students with learning disabilities and their parents should be asking.

I owe much of my knowledge to my good friend Dr. Susan Perez. She took a special interest in me in the sixth grade. We met at Thomas E. Weightman Middle School, through one of my good childhood friends. She was in her late 40s, her brown hair styled in loose body curls, and her skin the color of condensed milk. She was a doctoral student at the University of South Florida (USF) working on her dissertation regarding students with disabilities.

She introduced me to writing as a form of creative therapy. She took time to see something in me that others often overlooked. Her home became a safe haven for me. I often looked forward to spending time with Ms. Perez. I was amazed that she could type 99 words a minute without looking at the keys.

No matter what kind of emotional meltdown or behavior issues I was having she always knew how to reach me in a loving and supportive way.

She understood a lot of the hardships and systemic racism Black and Latino students endured while attending predominantly White institutions. She was the first person who taught me how to start flipping the label to make it work for me.

She helped identify and accept that my learning style is different, and that I may need some help at times, but there are other times when this label may be used to constrain my intellectual abilities, so I have to recognize when to flip the label.

One weekend before I had entered high school, she was driving me home from her house.

She told me, "When you and your mother go in for your IEP meeting, they are going to ask you, 'Do you want a special diploma? Tell them NO.

A special diploma is not good for anything. It is just a piece of paper saying you showed up for class every day for four years. You will not be able to go to college. Tanell, you **are** going to college. Make sure you say NO."

When Ms. Perez spoke to my mother that same night, she made sure my mother knew that same vital information.

She was the first educator to illustrate to me what an advocate for students with disabilities looked like. She never told me college *may* be an option for me. She always said that college *was* for me. She knew that with a college education, I could change my social location and my family's legacy. She never crossed the line to try to be my mother.

She respected the fact that I had a great mother who from time to time may have made unhealthy choices due to the disease of addiction that she struggled with.

My family and friends often tell me, "Tanell, you don't have a disability. You have three degrees, have traveled the world, and you have written a book. Some normal people haven't done that.

I have never known you to set a goal that you didn't accomplish for yourself. You say you're going to do it and you do." I humbly smile and say Thank you. Not because anything that I have accomplished is so great, but because through the power of faith, determination, dedication, and discipline I have consciously graduated from making the label work for me to flipping it, and now getting a seam ripper to remove the label off me that used to hinder, define, and limit me.

There was a point in my life when I had to flip the label in order to get access to the resources I needed. I did this by utilizing the extra help, time, and tutoring services that students with disabilities received. My specific disabilities allowed me to have time and a half to take tests and complete projects, use recording devices and audiobooks, and have a note-taker for classes.

We are socialized to believe that all labels are bad, but that is not always true. My being labeled as having a learning disability is not a bad thing in itself but labeling me as "other" and putting me and my abilities in a box, is.

Sometimes, stating what someone cannot or will not do can be like putting them in a box, or trying to put limits on them because their way of learning and processing material may be different. I had to tell myself the way I learn is different, the way I process information, or receive it does not fit into what mainstream educators and experts say I should.

I am a visual, verbal, audible, learner. I learn and process information better when I have more time to process my thoughts. I am highly intelligent. I am gifted and creative. I am more than capable, and competent enough to navigate and engineer my own learning style. My learning style fosters growth, understanding, knowledge, empowerment, productivity, and independence.

There are many others who have learning and emotional disabilities. I believe that if they were to be given the tools and opportunities needed to do more than survive with having a disability, they could thrive despite these challenges.

One of the greatest tools anyone can have is a loving and understanding support system to encourage them regardless of their circumstances. Some other tools are counseling and coaching that foster growth and self-efficacy. As a coach, I know firsthand how effective coaching and mentoring can be in becoming aware of one's learning style.

One of my mentors is Dr. Sharon Baker. She was the first Black woman that I personally knew who had a PhD, but not the last. In her mentoring me, she showed me what Black excellence looked like up close and personal. She planted seeds of greatness in me, that dared me to dream past the small sleepy town that I resided in.

In many ways, she has never stopped mentoring me. She is often a fountain of wisdom and a voice of reasoning. Dr. Baker is literally a global traveler. She is always traveling and expanding her social location. She gave me permission to do the same unapologetically. In fact, she prepared me for my second trip abroad years later. I will never forget her reaction when I told her, "I am going to China for a year."

She replied, "Wow! Mocha, that is great. I just left China. You need to know that some of the women I went with did not like it because they were on the heavier side and darker they felt discriminated against."

Wide-eyed, I replied, "Really!"

She replied, "Yes, so be prepared to face some discrimination based on your size and the color of your skin."

She prepared me to walk through the door of my next international experience while minimizing some of the blow of culture shock and discrimination she knew I would face, as a plus-sized, dark-skinned African American woman.

In my eyes, there is nothing more liberating than a Black woman holding the door open for another Black woman to walk through. Dr. Baker honestly did this through mentoring us. She was so classy, well-polished, and poised at everything she did. Ms. Foutain was a sociology professor at ECC who also mentored us. They illustrated to the group of Black women that they mentored, on the importance of sisterhood and unity. Through their mentoring, they took time to show me that I am an audio and dialog learner. I learn better when I am able to hear and engage with the material I am learning.

Dr. Black, my theater professor, taught me how to think analytically and critically about the information I was learning even when studying the arts. He taught me the importance of time management, timeliness, honesty, and that the arts are creative, but also an outlet for expression. In doing so, he challenged me to think about everything I was being taught, process it, and then give my own analytical opinion. He was the mentor I never saw coming!

Marta Walz, my speech coach, taught me how to bring all of me to my speaking platforms when I spoke. She made me believe when I spoke I was operating in my purpose and that was bigger than any label anyone could put on me. She taught me as a speaker I have to be honest, direct, and clear when researching and delivering my speeches. To always find the sources that affirm and validate the information I am presenting. To do my very best, to have fun, to be a person of honor, and integrity. Yet as my speech coach she opened me up to new experiences and taught me life is about gaining new experiences.

Before joining the speech team, when I went out to eat, I ate the same things: burgers, fries, and hot wings. I did not realize how boxed in I was until one time after the team decided to eat dinner at a Mexican restaurant. I was sitting there with an attitude the size of the state of Montana because they were pushing me out of my comfort zone.

As I looked over the menu, I found myself getting extremely upset. When my food came out, I was extremely irritated because in my mind I felt like they burned my food on top of me hating to try anything different. My chicken looked a little too dark-skinned for me in some places, however I now know that it was cooked properly. Everyone at my table could tell by the look on my face I was not happy.

Marta quickly assisted me with finding another option but affirmed my efforts of trying something new. Being a part of a national winning speech team exposed me to opportunities to travel and woke up a desire in me to experience more cultures and countries abroad.

Her coaching style affirmed me in many ways and fostered an atmosphere of positive self-efficacy.

I remembered her encouraging me to wear my large hoops that were bigger than the size of a nickel, and her being OK with my burgundy, naturally curly hair. The smile that lit up her face when she saw it was so affirming. My personal style was not encouraged in speaking competitions. Your earrings should be no bigger than a nickel, and they encourage you to have modest hairstyles. Nothing in your face, pull back, sleek, and professional looking. She was an excellent coach.

Coaching is essential because it deals with positive psychology; as a coach you never tell your clients what to do. You ask them powerful questions that give the keys to unlock what they may need, by walking with them on their journey and holding them accountable. Marta used positive psychology to allow me to choose how I would depict myself as a speaker, as opposed to allowing the label of forensic speaker to define how I showed up to live out my purpose. I think she also knew asking me to change it would stifle my creative and unique voice.

For far too long we have allowed labels to define and confine us. In many ways becoming the prisons that legislate others' limitations that were placed on us.

Dr. Susan Perez asserts, "I don't like the label 'disability'; it makes students feel ashamed, stupid, and embarrassed. I never knew a student in special ed. that was not embarrassed by that label. The system makes the students feel like they failed when really, the system has failed them. It makes students feel like there is something wrong with them because these labels don't take into account that everyone learns differently.``

It is disheartening when we allow others' opinions and thoughts to become our own perceptions and beliefs about ourselves. Being in the wrong environment, being fostered by the wrong people, and having the wrong perception of yourself can cause you to stay stagnant and deny you access to soaring.

I remember hearing the fable about the little eagle who thought he was a chicken. I thought to myself, "Wow, this is powerful!"

This baby eagle was hanging around with chickens because he was rescued by a farmer who found him before he hatched and placed him in a chicken coop. Since he was raised by a hen, he thought he was a chicken. He was walking, clucking, confessing, and acting like a chicken because of the label that was placed on him.

I imagined that even though he looked nothing like a chicken, he was labeled as a chicken because he was raised and nurtured in the chicken coop. He may have even had some of the mannerisms of chickens from spending so much time around them. They labeled him as a chicken for so long that he began to act like a chicken and suppress his real identity.

I grew up in the south in a place where it is common to see cows on the side of the road and pigs here or there. You can even see what my Great-Great-Granny-Granny would call "yard birds," or chickens. Yard Birds, mmm! It's funny how the young eagle had been reduced to a simple, clueless chicken, with limited experience, and a short life expectancy.

Maybe you are an eagle, but because you have been labeled a chicken, and have spent so much time around chickens, you have stopped being and believing in who you really are and what you were uniquely created to do.

This is a great example of why there are some labels we must reject. When labels hinder, restrict, oppress, deprive, and limit us; they are toxic. Anything that affects you negatively, or goes against your divine identity, you must courageously remove from yourself.

When an older and wiser eagle came along and removed the label that was attached to the young eagle, the young eagle was able to embrace its innate and divine identity, as opposed to accepting its learned and fostered identity. It is mind-boggling how one wrong label, or simply a bad thought, can change one's perspective of oneself. Was it a chicken, or was it an eagle? Once the little eagle knew and believed that it was an eagle, it began to fly and behave like an eagle because it no longer accepted the label that identified it as chicken. It knew it was meant to soar.

Ask yourself this powerful question: **Am I ready to soar?** If so, my friend, get ready to experience 1 Corinthians 2:9: "Eye hath not seen, nor ear heard. Neither has it entered the heart of man, the things which God hath prepared for them that love Him." ***It is your time to soar!** You were made for this!*

Pearls of Wisdom

Taking the Labels Off

- You have the right to remove any label that does not correctly identify you or restricts your purpose.
- You can flip the label and make it work for you, or get a seam ripper and remove it.
- Never allow the labels of others to define or limit you.
- "You can never soar with eagles, as long as you are hanging out with the turkeys."
- Knowing your identity is essential to fulfilling your purpose.
- Taking labels off requires you to put in the work, to overcome them.
- Identify who is the best advocate for you and trust their advice pertaining to you.
- Never be afraid or intimidated to ask questions when it comes to matters that affect you.
- Give yourself permission to use the creative and performing arts as a form of therapy.

Chapter 4

My Baby Leaped

> "Every great move forward in your life begins with
> a leap of faith, a step into the unknown."
>
> —Brian Tracy

My baby leaped! Once I overheard my class valedictorian saying that she was going to attend Spelman College. I did not know anything about Spelman, but something in the pit of my stomach leaped and told me that this was where I was supposed to attend college. But with my ACT results, the idea of going to Spelman College seemed like a joke. I wondered to myself, *What college would really look at me as a potential student?* I settled for going to hair school because doing hair was something I was good at, it was a skill I could get paid for, and I had been accepted to Truman College Technical Center.

On my first day of attending cosmetology school, my teacher said, "Look to your left and to your right. Some of you *guys* are not going to make it." I'd seen and heard this before many years ago as I was watching "A Different World," a popular TV show. Like so many other African Americans, I grew up loving and tuning in on Thursday nights to watch The *Cosby Show* and *A Different World*. These shows had a very positive impact on the African American community. They depicted some of the pros and cons of college life for minority students, yet always offered hope during each segment.

They discussed topics such as gun violence, gender equality, domestic violence, mental health, classism, racism, and sizeism. They personally made me feel as if with a college degree I could experience a different world. I never forgot Malcolm X's quote because of "A Different World," "Education is the passport to the future, for tomorrow belongs to those who prepare for it today."

I heard my cosmetology teacher's words and pondered them. I have always had a strong spirit of discernment; I knew that she thought I would be one of those people who was not going to make it, but "The devil is a liar, and so is his mother-in-law!" At the same time, a part of me felt sure that she was not talking about me because I knew within me that I was going to finish what I started.

I wondered what kind of opposition I would have to endure to graduate. A thought came to my mind as I sat quietly in the tan and chrome metal desk chair surrounded by other African American women and two men, all of us fighting within ourselves in the same internal battle praying and silently saying to one another, "I am not going to be one of the 'some of you who are not going to make it.'" What was the point of this speech, was it to warn us, or to challenge us to come out swinging against the odds of not making it?

I studied my cosmetology teacher's beautiful face, trying to guess her age. She was simply beautiful, intelligent, skillful, sassy, and full of wisdom. She was tall and thin, with skin the perfect color of light caramelized toffee. Her hair was jet black.

Every blue moon you would see a of couple strands of gray hair trying to reveal her age. It was not until I saw a picture of her husband that I realized that she had to be at least 55.

She walked fast, moved fast, and could read through nonsense even faster. She was always a breath of fresh air and encouraged us to excel as stylists. We called her *Smittie* behind her back. It did not take her long to access our skill set.

One day in class I recited a poem. After hearing me Smittie remarked "Wow Tanell, I did not know you had all of that in you. I am proud of you." Right before we graduated, she came up to me and apologized to me. "You know, Tanell, I really owe you an apology. I really did not think you were going to make it. I am sorry for doubting you." She did not offend me. All my life people have underestimated me until they got to know and witness my work ethic, hard work, and sheer determination to fight against the odds that had been dealt to me.

I knew what Curtis Jackson, aka 50 Cent meant when he said, "I'mma get rich, or die trying." Les Brown poetically captures what 50 Cent meant when he flipped Berton Braley's poem titled "The Will to Win " on its head. In doing so he delivers this powerful message with motivational blow after blow, punching certain words for dramatic pause.

If you want a thing bad enough, to go out and fight for it,

To workday and night for it,

To give up your time, peace, and sleep for it,

If all that you dream and scheme is about it,

And life seems useless and worthless without it

If you will gladly sweat for it and fret for it and plan for it

And lose all your terror of opposition for it.

If you simply go after this thing that you want with all your capacity, strength, and sagacity.

Faith hope and confidence and stern pertinacity

If neither cold, poverty, famine, nor gout

Sickness nor pain of body and brain

Can keep you away from the thing you want.

If dogged and grim you besiege and beset it,

[With the help of God,] you will get it!

This poem perfectly depicts my drive to accomplish my goals, my dreams, and my life's purpose through God. I may not have the highest IQ or the greatest skill set, but I have learned to use what I do have in my hand to get what I want and need not just to survive, but to thrive in life. I know how to fight for what I want. When I want something, I go after it with all I have. My drive, my passion, and my desire then become this poem in motion, and nothing "can keep [me] away from the thing [I] want."

Pearls of Wisdom

My Baby Leaped

- ➤ Your baby is that thing that gives life to your purpose, or your life purpose.
- ➤ You are giving birth to your baby/ whose purpose is bigger than you, and bigger than how you feel in each trimester.
- ➤ When your baby leaps, it is a reminder that there is still hope, life, and purpose attached to it.
- ➤ When your baby leaps, write it down.
- ➤ When pregnant with a baby/ purpose you must give birth at the right time.
- ➤ Never stop fanning the flame of your purpose or encouraging your baby to leap by faith.

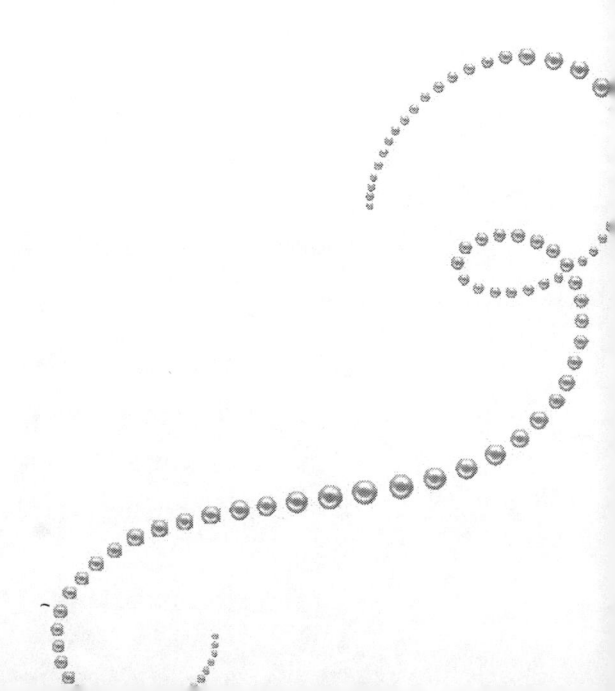

Chapter 5

Tearing Down My Rocky Foundation

> *Then the Lord put forth his hand and touched my mouth. And the Lord said unto me, Behold, I have put my words in thy mouth. See, I have this day set thee over the nations and over the kingdoms, to root out, and to pull down, and to destroy, and to throw down, to build, and to plant.*
>
> —*Jeremiah 1:9-10 (KJV)*

I started attending Elgin Community College (ECC) during the Spring of 2003. I was 23 years old. I had been working in a salon for five years and loved helping people feel better about themselves. Yet there was a void in my life only higher education could fill. Though I was attending ECC, I had recently applied to Judson College, in Elgin IL.

I was standing outside in the blistering summer heat. I had just taken the bus to ECC to promote my upcoming spoken word event. As I walked down the cool hallways, I could feel the AC gently kissing my warm-to-the-touch skin. As I walked down the long hallway, I heard the Holy Spirit say, "You *are not going to attend Judson College; you are going to go here for two years and then transfer to Spelman.*" I spoke up audibly, and said, "The devil is a liar! I am going to Judson College*.*"

Later, when I received my letter from Judson College's admissions office, I was so excited to read it. I had been stalking our mail carrier.

It was a warm sunny day in Elgin, yet I remember it not being extremely hot. There was a gentle cool breeze blowing. I started walking to the mailbox barefoot as I always did.

My family thinks I am so country for walking around barefoot and they are right. I am so country and proud of it. With everything hanging and swinging on me, I quickly snuck out the front door braless and shoeless to retrieve my mail.

The pavement was silently cool under my feet, but as I walked down the carport, the pavement began to heat up.

As I pulled open the silver metal mailbox, a wave of adrenaline rushed within me. I knew I needed to rip this letter open as quickly as possible.

More than anything, I craved privacy at this moment. Most of my family was gone and the house was quiet, but I still needed to be alone with just me and God to see what this letter was going to say. I walked into the main bathroom on the first floor and locked the door behind me. I sat on the cool porcelain toilet, fully dressed. I flipped the letter over and tore it open. As I read the letter in silence, my eyes began to sting. I reached the portion of the letter stating that they felt it would be better for me to attend a community college first and maintain a 2.5 GPA for at least a semester before considering me as a candidate for applying to their institution.

I gasped, "The nerve of them." *Not only was I not accepted, you want to try to tell me what you want me to do to possibly get accepted to your crummy school. I didn't like your damn school anyway.*

I was so hurt and disappointed. The truth of the matter is that I did want to go to Judson College, but for all the wrong reasons. I wanted to go because that is where other people told me I should apply to, it was a good school, it was local, and because it was a four-year school, it was better than ECC.

Judson was never my first choice, but somewhere along the line I allowed myself to believe it was my only option. I stopped caring whether or not it was the best option for me. I was not going to ECC. I was above going to someone's junior college. Who would have known going to that junior college would literally change my life for the better? I can honestly say, I never thought that, but it did change my life for the better and taught me to never "...despise small beginnings."

I sat and cried about the reality of someone else's dream for me slipping through my fingers. Holy Spirit began to encourage, instruct, and remind me of God's plan for my life. Holy Spirit brought back to my recollection what God had told me, that I was going to attend ECC for two years, and then transfer to Spelman College.

I wanted to share with my Auntie Jewel what had happened, but the Holy Spirit told me not to. I could not share with anyone that I was not accepted. Not because I was ashamed, but because God had not released me to share about it. My Auntie is a natural nurturer. She would coddle me through the grieving process of not getting accepted to Judson College.

God wanted me to trust Him, and how He was leading and nurturing in this process, to showcase His glory.

A month or more had passed and I was at our family's church. The Holy Spirit had torn that place apart. It was not the meeting room at the Days Inn. It had been transformed into a place of worship, where the presence of "The Most-High" was welcomed. The atmosphere was always charged with the presence of God. I began to testify about God's divine timing, the purpose for which God had called me, and the Hand of God transforming my life.

I was walking through the hallways of ECC and God told me, *You are going to go here for two years and transfer to Spelman.*

I said, *'The devil is a liar, I am going to Judson.'*

It is funny how we think we know what is best for us. We busy ourselves making plans for our lives outside the divine will and purpose of God. See, what God was really asking me was, *Tanell, do you trust me with your purpose and your future when it does not look like what you made plans for it to be? Do you believe that even during a detour, you can give birth to your purpose? Do you trust me?*

I knew who God was, and yes, I did trust him to take me on a detour. He said, *"I am getting ready to shape your faith through all of this."* I had applied to Judson College, and I did not get in.

At the time it was something I could not share with anyone because I needed God to help me deal with that level of disappointment.

I don't know who I am talking to.

There are some rejections and pain that you must go through with you and God. I heard the Holy Spirit say that Judson College was not a part of my purpose. *You are going to ECC and You are going to transfer to Spelman.*

Sometimes the very thing, the very person, and the very situation that we were crying loudly about was never meant to be a part of our future. I said all this to say, God's divine timing and plan is always the best one. Trust the process; I promise, you will not regret it.

Elgin Community College was a place of breaking and remaking for me. It was a place where I learned how to be a student. Without my ECC experience, I would not have been prepared to attend Spelman. I would've flunked out my first semester.

I learned so much about myself as a woman, as a person, and as a student at ECC. I started this club called "Sassy Girl," which fostered positive self-esteem and self-efficacy for plus-size women. I thought it was just going to be a place for me to have a safe haven and help other women become more confident and their true selves, but to my surprise women of all sizes wanted to become a part of "Sassy Girl," because of what it stood for.

Some women who were skinny said I want to be a part of "Sassy Girl!"' I need to work on my self-confidence too. I need to work on my self-esteem and things I want to improve about myself. My mission then became making "Sassy Girl," into an official club at the community college. "Sassy Girl" is still an official club at ECC today.

We did community service events, such as making and donating Easter baskets for a low-income daycare. We provided hot meals for families with financial difficulties for Thanksgiving. We gave Christmas gifts to the children within our community.

"Sassy Girl" became more than just a club to me. It was a place where I could tell the world, forget you, if you think my standard of beauty is ugly, everywhere we look in mainstream society we are conditioned to believe that thin is the ideal. They tried to tell us what beauty was supposed to look like when beauty is truly in the eye of the beholder. I learned as a plus-size woman that my curves are beautiful and the way I walk into a room and take charge of it is something phenomenal.

I guess that's why Dr. Angelou wrote the poem "Phenomenal Woman." At ECC, I learned that I am phenomenal in the skin that I am in and to never be apologetic for being my authentic self. I also learned how to find my voice as a speaker by being on its award-winning speech team. This changed my life in so many ways. It opened me up to new experiences, and I was able to travel the country, competing in forensic speaking, learn about different topics, and converse with diverse people who want to change the world.

My theater professor, Dr. Black, was an interesting fellow. He taught me how to write and how to defend my opinion.

He urged, "Mocha, you have something to say, and you need to say it to the world. The only way you're going to be able to say it is to say it and defend your opinions and your actions with documentation, elaborating, citing your sources, and clearly articulating what and why you are saying what you are saying."

I will never forget Dr. Black and all the lessons that he taught me while ECC was my stomping ground and not just any stomping ground, but a steppingstone to the greatness that God wanted to launch me into.

I learned how to be a student, how to study, and how to engage in extracurricular activities while honing my purpose. One time, I was stressed out, I was taking 17 credit hours as a full-time student, while being on a speech team, engaged in ministry, living on my own, and working two part-time jobs. By the end of the semester, I was overwhelmed and stressed out. Dr. Black encouraged me, saying, "Mocha keep going. You are almost at the finish line."

You need people to cheer you on. They can see that you are barely holding on and they come along and motivate you to keep going. I remember telling someone once, "I am at the end of my rope, and I don't have any more rope to hang on to." They replied, "That's what faith is. When you do not have any more rope left, you tie an invisible knot, and you hold on tighter with faith. My entire journey at ECC was a *faith walk* and a voyage of self-discovery.

I learned that I had something to say and that I could express myself well through poetry. I won and placed in a couple of poetry slams while attending ECC. It made me feel like I could take on the world. Creatively, I was a force to reckon with due to my poetic style.

When I first started attending ECC, I had to take remedial classes. Dr. Black told me that my writing was not at college level and that I had slipped through a crack in the educational system. That professor did not tear me down and just leave me there; he helped rebuild my academic foundation.

I left his office with two options. I could give up on my dream of a higher education, or I could come out swinging against the odds that had been dealt to me my entire life. I went from an A to a D in his class. I retook his class a couple of semesters later and earned an A.

I remember the first day in his class the second time around. I sat there determined to be successful but wary of his opinion of me, uncertain whether he would give me a chance to redeem myself.

As our class sat in a circle, he passed out white flash cards, blank on one side and striped on the other side. He instructed us to write our name on the card, what we preferred to be called, and why we were taking this class."

I said, *"Hello, my name is Tanell Vashawn Allen. You can call me Mocha. This is my second time taking this class. I hope you won't hold my past against my future."*

Words cannot express how that one statement changed my life. Dr. Black created an open-door policy to critique all my papers for his class before I officially turned them in. He encouraged me multiple times when I felt like giving up. He was my first professor to ever read my poetry. He thought I could turn them into songs.

I had been torn down by so many people in my life that I became conditioned to believe all criticism was negative, rather than constructive. When he pulled me to the side that day, I was defensive, and my emotions were high. I felt that he was not trying to help me become a better student; he was literally on an assignment from Satan himself to crush my dream and self-esteem.

I took this to a new level of spiritual warfare. Stressing myself out all because I didn't know how to take constructive criticism that was meant to inspire me to be better, not bitter.

Looking back over that situation, I am truly grateful to Dr. Black. He cared enough about me to be honest, patient, and to teach me how to become an analytical writer. Who knows, maybe he is part of the reason I am an author today.

Dr. Black wrote me a letter of recommendation to Spelman College, and I was accepted.

May 9, 2007

Spelman College

Tanell Allen
104 Woodland Court Apt #1 A
Carpentersville, IL 60110

Dear Ms. Allen:

On behalf of the Spelman College Admissions Committee, it is my privilege to extend to you this invitation to enroll into the Spelman community of scholars beginning with the Fall 2007 semester. Congratulations! Each year we have the difficult task of choosing from the many applications received, a limited number of transfer students. In presenting these congratulations, please know that they are sincere and well deserved.

Your selection is an indication of our recognition of the excellence you have demonstrated by your academic record and the spirit you have presented through your community and civic involvement. As you know, Spelman College is a place where young women enter with a potential to operate in leadership roles and graduate with the tools to serve through the realization of that potential. We have faith that you will continue in that tradition.

During the next few weeks, I expect that you will want to know more about the next steps to becoming a student here at Spelman.

The information enclosed with this letter should be a good beginning to finding some of the answers you may need. great care in selecting the students invited to enter the College.

In reviewing our facilities and our programs as they relate to the goals, interests, and talents presented in your application, I am certain that this is a great match.

I know that transferring from one college to another means more than just changing campuses. You are leaving friends and a very special community to join ours. I want to make this transition one that is as seamless and positive as possible. Please feel free to contact me at 1-800-982-2411 if there is anything I, or anyone at the College, can do to assist you in the process. We are very much looking forward to your arrival and wish you all the best in the meantime.

Sincerely,

Arlene Vice

Pearls of Wisdom

Tearing Down My Rocky Foundation

- There is a difference between criticism and constructive criticism.
- Make sure you do not allow your feelings to cloud great advice.
- Push yourself to be the best version of yourself regardless of what others think of you.
- Remember that the tearing down process may hurt, but that it will make you better than you were before.
- Some critics are really your Pushers in disguise.
- Everyone deserves a second chance or do-over.
- The thing that is said or done that hurts the most may have some truth to it.
- Never adopt other people's dreams as your own.
- Always trust God's divine plans for life.

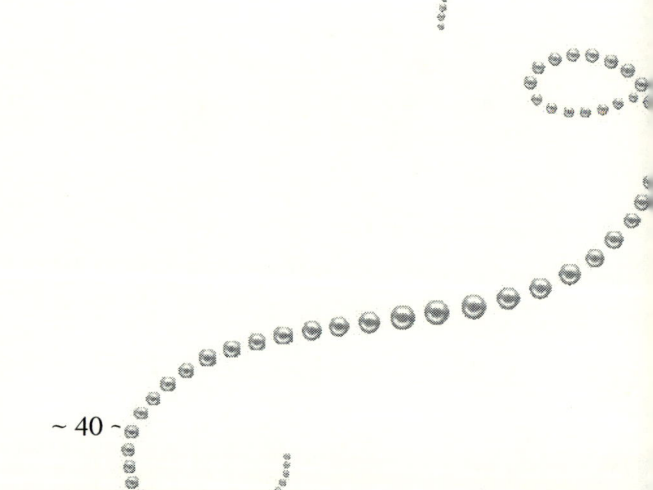

Chapter 6

I am a Dreamer

> "A Dreamer is a visionary who dares to dream against the odds.
>
> —Tanell Vashawn Allen M.Div.

All my life, I have been a Dreamer in some ways. I think it helped me cope with the reality of my home life. I am the product of a broken home where my mother was a domestic violence victim and sexual assault survivor, trying her best to cope with the traumas she had experienced most of her life. These traumas led to her becoming a teenage mother, stuck in an abusive marriage with an older man. My mother finally left my father, but the years of abuse she suffered left her physically and emotionally scarred.

After, divorcing my father, my mother met my youngest brother's father, who introduced her to drugs. For years, she struggled with an addiction until she was able to learn how to take her voice back. I consider my mother a real badass because she has overcome so much through God's grace and mercy. She was the first person who nourished my dreams, and she did it despite her circumstances.

As a kid, I would prance in front of the mirror and speak over myself. I always saw myself doing something great. In my mind and spirit, I could always hear myself preaching, speaking, and encouraging others. One day, I opened my mouth and began preaching to myself.

I am a Dreamer; I am the Joseph or the "Jo-Jo" of my family. I always have been a ball of positivity and optimism. "I choose to always see the glass half full as opposed to half empty."

Not many people choose to look at life through the lens of optimism. Life has left them jaded. They no longer believe in themselves, or in others. They have allowed the dream that God gave them to die. They no longer dream or are seen as dreamers.

Somewhere the dream died and caused a part of the Dreamer to die along with it. Mirroring the effect of the death of a loved one, a relationship, or a job. How one never quite recovers from that emotional trauma. It is a terrible thing to see a Dreamer lose their ability to dream. You will see the fire in their eyes leave their soul. The passion that inspires and cultivates will turn into empty words and the one thing that they lived for will become the thing they dread the most.

Joseph's name means the one who adds. His brothers were so envious of him that they wanted to kill him. You can kill the Dreamer, but you cannot kill the dream, or the movement God wants to bring forth on the Earth.

We saw this with John the Baptist being beheaded, we saw this with Jesus being crucified, Perpetua being martyred, Martin Luther King Jr. being assassinated, and **Breonna Taylor being murdered**. All of these Dreamers died, but their dreams, missions, and goals continue to live on.

Most people don't realize that every dream has to go through the process of being cultivated in order to fully come to fruition. Dr. Myles Monroe, the late evangelist and author, reflected that "every seed had to be buried in the dirt in order to grow." Timing and dying to oneself is a must for one to give birth to one's dream.

Scholars estimate that there was about a thirteen-year period during which Joseph was put in a pit and had many trials before he reigned over Egypt. Sometimes as Dreamers we stop dreaming because of the challenges we face, as Dr. Apostle Dexter Ball asserted in his sermon "From the Pit to the Palace." It would have been easy for Joseph to become fed up waiting for the dream to come to pass.

He could have blamed his brothers for putting him in the pit. He could have slept with Potiphar's wife because she was throwing herself at him.

He could have been angry for having been wrongly convicted and sentenced to prison. He could have been bitter because the Butler did not do what he said he was going to do when they got out of prison. He said he would put in a good word to the King, but he did not. He got out of jail and his help turned out to be simply "jail talk." All this simply played a part in making the Dreamer into a leader.

As leaders we have people who are assigned to us and hired for certain tasks. Some may even volunteer to perform or do things that never get done. As leaders we cannot become bitter toward them, hold grudges, or simply cut them off. We must learn how to resolve this conflict in a mature and reasonable manner.

There is always going to be somebody who will disappoint us. Disappointment is essential in learning how to deal with conflict and become solution oriented. It was essential for Joseph to be developed as a leader because a Dreamer is also a visionary who has insight into how to lead.

Although Joseph was a natural leader his character had to be developed under pressure and the hard knocks of life. Show me a leader whose character has not been developed under pressure and I will show you a prideful and narcissistic leader who leads by their emotions and ego.

In 1999 my dream was to attend Spelman College. But it did not happen until 2007. During this time my study habits and characters were being shaped to prepare me to be a Spelman Woman.

If I had not gone through those years of preparation just as Joseph did, I would not have made it to Spelman College, or I would have flunked or dropped out during my first semester due to the pressure to perform at a level I was not quite ready for.

Have you ever stopped and wondered why it took the Butler so long to recall the promise he made to Joseph to remember him when he was released? Maybe the Butler truly forgot about him, or maybe Josepth was right on time with his divine appointment, of being shaped into a leader.

Pearls of Wisdom

I Am a Dreamer

- Never allow the dream to die or hit the ground.
- Build a team or a tribe to support you and hold you accountable.
- Never share your dream with small-minded people.
- Never allow others to talk you out doing what is best for you.
- Give yourself permission to be selfish, or to choose yourself first when it comes to achieving the goals and dreams that line up with your purpose.
- You cannot give what you do not have, so take time for self-care and advancing yourself.
- Remember that not everyone is going to be happy about your dreams and goals, so be protective of them and use discernment in sharing them.
- Every Dreamer must go through the pit and the prison to get to the palace.
- Every Dreamer has the potential to be a great leader if they allow themselves to become developed.
- As a Dreamer you cannot afford to play it small or safe. People are waiting on you to ignite the greatness within them.
- Dreamers are change agents—catalysts for change.

- Leaders are not born; they are developed through the rigors of life's assignments.

- A Dreamer's dreams are often the blueprint of God's divine purpose for their life.

- Never forget that God is the Dream-Giver and that without Him we can do nothing.

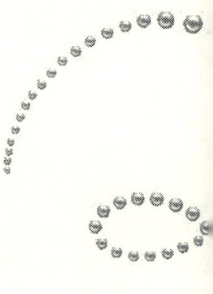

Chapter 7

Crying in the Closet

> *A strong person is not the person who doesn't cry. A strong person is the one who cries and sheds tears for the moment, then gets up and fights again.*
>
> —*iliketoquote.com*

I wish I could tell you that my struggle with learning became easier with each degree I earned but it did not. Even with my academic achievements, I often felt as if I was illiterate. I always shortchanged myself when it came to valuing my intellectual abilities. Although I knew I worked extremely hard to excel, the voice of self-sabotage always credited my success to perseverance and not intellect. I never felt smart enough, or competent enough, for certain intellectual jobs that would stretch me as a person.

When I wrote my first book, "Let the Church Say Amen: Confessions of a Single Minister," I struggled with my confidence and my writing skills. I realized that in some ways I was too embarrassed to share it with the world. Content-wise, I knew my book was special.

That readers would be blown away by my storytelling skills, inspired, and entertained; yet the idea of everyone seeing and reading my work scared me. No matter how many times I proofread or had others edit my book, I believed people would read it and discover how ignorant I was.

That my academic peers from grad school would call each other to gossip with each other about how I tried to write a book but it was littered with typos, grammatical mistakes, and fragmented sentences.

I was so concerned about how others would perceive me and my book that it was difficult to celebrate the accomplishment of completing it. A good friend had to spend a lot of time encouraging me to celebrate this noteworthy life achievement of becoming a published author. *Why can't I just get it?* I ask myself. I am slightly envious of intellectual people who just get things the first time around. Many people do not know how many days I spent crying in the closet because I just could not figure it out.

I recall one of my assignments back during my first semester at ECC. I had worked on it all night, but it somehow didn't save onto my computer. I searched and searched my computer, but it was gone. I had stayed up all night long fighting through my fears and anxiety of working on my paper for class. And at the last moment, it was ***gone.***

Some people do not realize that having an intellectual disability is something you never really get over, you always feel its effects. You adjust and learn different habits that help you become successful. You learn to cope with a myriad of challenges.

There were days I cried and prayed just to be normal, to be able to understand like other people.

God, why do I have to read things so many times? In the past I would have to read over material six and seven times before I understood it. I often questioned internally and externally, Why am I so slow at everything? The worst part about was that others might run circles around what it took me hours to do, in less than half the time, and it likely would still be better than what I had done.

Here I was, faced with this paper I still had to write. I was so overwhelmed and frustrated by anxiety over fear of failure. This caused me enormous stress. My fear of failure often stopped me from trying.

When writing academic papers, I never really knew where to start, so I would procrastinate until I had no other choice but to make myself do the work. And then, I would pretty much have to binge and cram to get everything done. Stress, fear, adrenaline, and time pushed me to get it done.

I had three severe mental and emotional breakdowns while working on this very paper. I was taking English 098 an intermediate class in the Spring of 2003 and this particular breakdown left me crying in the closet. I was so mad, frustrated, and ashamed. The next morning was a morning from hell. My paper was due, and I had nothing. It was gone. I shook my head in disbelief. **VANISHED! NOOOOO! NO! NO! This cannot be happening!**

I knew within me the slightest thing would send me over the edge. I remember crying and not wanting any of my family to hear me. Which was next to impossible with the nine people who were usually living in our house. We were beyond what was known as a blended family.

My auntie had three kids, she took in me and two of my other cousins, a spiritual son, and she and my uncle made our family total a whopping nine. At times ten when my uncle's daughter came over.

This time it was different. There were only three people home this morning. My Auntie Jewel was a very light sleeper. On top of my paper getting lost, I was running late, and someone had forgotten to restart the dryer, which they had opened, leaving *my clothes* still wet. I **lost it**. I shut myself in the closet and began to cry.

Hot tears poured down my face, soaking my stained housedress. My body began to tremble violently in response to my emotional distress. I felt flushed as another wave of emotions washed over my body. I yelled within myself, *GOD, WHY? WHY AM I NOT SMART? WHY DO I HAVE TO STRUGGLE?* I wiped the mixture of snot and tears away with the back of my hand, just as I heard my aunt ask, "Who is that?"

I did not want her to know it was me. I tried to silence myself, but it was as if the floodgates had opened. I got quieter, but anyone who listened closely enough could still hear my soft whimpering. I thought my aunt went back to sleep, but she did not.

She called out moments later, "Who is that with that doggone crying? Mocha-Tanell?"

I responded, "Yeah Auntie."

She said, "Come here."

I walked into my aunt and uncle's room, to my aunt turned halfway over, with her head leaning in the direction of the door. When she saw me, she rolled over and sat up, adjusting her beautiful hazel eyes to see me clearly and to discern my emotional distress.

She asked, "Nell-girl, what's wrong with you?"

I let everything out quickly and stormed off to my room. I was still crying moments later when I heard my Auntie walking up towards me to comfort me and to stop me from crying alone in my closet.

Pearls of Wisdom

Crying in the Closet

- ➢ Meet with an advocate, or team member to make sure you understand what is being asked of or required of you.
- ➢ Tape instructions so you can replay them for clarity.
- ➢ Start projects early and give yourself fake deadlines so you will not miss the real ones.
- ➢ Arrive fifteen to thirty minutes early to ask questions.
- ➢ Take advantage of office hours, coaching, and mentorships.
- ➢ Never hide in the closet out of shame or fear of being rejected.
- ➢ Always save and backup your work.
- ➢ Never allow the fear of failure to stop you from trying.

Chapter 8

I am Your Pusher

> *I'm a Pusher dealing hope, at the intersection of desire and despair.*
>
> —*Unknown*

Who is Your Pusher? Who is that person, that thing, that idea that helps you cultivate the greatness inside of you when all hell breaks loose and you are hanging out in the valley of despair and depression? Who is that one person who can make you come out swinging against the challenges, or odds? The one who is able to inspire you to keep going when you have run out of gas, and you know you are just barely making it on fumes. The person with whom one conversation unlocks the greatness dormant within you.

The funny thing about Your Pusher is that often they may not look, sound, act, or seem like they would be the one to help you raise your momentum. One Pusher I had was like this. Her name was Gail Shadwell. She was a speech professor at ECC. When I met Ms. Shadwell, I suffered from crippling depression and low self-efficacy.

She was White, tall, full-figured, plain-Jane looking, with short, thin salt-and-pepper hair. She was full of poise and wisdom, the kind of soul that people naturally gravitate to for strength, wisdom, encouragement, and laughter.

I will never forget what she told me one day when I was struggling with my self-efficacy.

"Women of our stature have a presence about us when we walk into a room, and when we open our mouth to speak."

The truth is I knew others thought I was a gifted orator, but somewhere within I still questioned if I was good enough.

I had been doing public speaking since the eighth grade and performing spoken word poetry since the ninth grade.

The only time I did not feel totally invisible was when I opened my mouth to speak. There was something about my presence when I began to speak that made the world stand back and take notice. That very same world that underestimated, judged, and stereotyped me as being a certain way had to stand back and take notice of me.

I feared that at any moment my audience would discover I am not that great of a speaker, that it's only my passion and delivery that creates an illusion. I spent my entire childhood in speech therapy and still had a slight lisp. How was I going to be a great orator? I won most of my competitions because of my hard work and dedication to my craft as a speaker. The hours practicing in front of the mirror, taping my speeches, listening to them again, and again, and again. Hearing my mother's voice telling me to say it again. All of this is what pushed me into becoming a skilled orator.

I questioned, *How did I earn a full scholarship to compete in forensic speaking?*

The truth is that I put in the work. I never sought to apply for a forensic speaking speech scholarship. It was my Intro to Speech professor, Mrs. Grice, who saw something in me and decided to be my Pusher.

When I gave my first speech in class, I tried to hide the slight nervous tremble in my voice. I was no longer speaking at church or at a conference hall. When my right hand began to tremble, I hid it behind my back.

Mrs. Grice came up to me after class and began to tell me how well I did. Tanell you are a gifted speaker. You did a really good job."

I replied, "Thank you, but I was really nervous."

A month or so into the class she told me, "Tanell you should join the speech team. One of the perks of being on the team is that you can earn a two-year scholarship."

I replied, "Really!" I was not that keen about being on the team, but I was more than excited about receiving a full ride to college.

When I first joined ECC's speech team, I thought we were going to be speaking in this big auditorium in front of a lot of people, but to my surprise, we competed with five of our peers in front of three or four judges. If you placed high enough in a round you were able to advance another round.

Even though the competitions were small and intimate, we competed in college rooms, or some hotel rooms once we got to the nationals. You were always learning something about a particular topic that was shared in that round; then taking it back to your community, your school, your family and friend circles, and having polite conversations about it.

At times those conversations were not so polite and they were not so nice but were needed to provoke and evoke change.

I remember doing a speech on intra-racism and talking about the brown paperback theory and how a lot of us still suffer from racism within one's race. I also did a communication analysis speech that analyzed how Bill Cosby was trying to make African Americans into the model minority with his Brown vs. Board of Education speech. I also did pros storytelling. I told the story of Alice Walker and how she lost an eye while her brothers were playing cowboys and Indians with a BB gun.

I loved being on the speech team. It taught me to be poised and confident, but most of all, it taught me how to be a better communicator. Something about me competing on the speech team did wonders for my self-esteem and self-efficacy. It made me believe that I could be and do anything, and the full ride for my college tuition that came with my scholarship was very beneficial too. This is when I met Marta Walz, my speech coach, who was simply amazing.

Marta ignited something in everyone that made us want to strive for greatness. She made sure we spoke on topics we were passionate about. A person of integrity, Marta allowed me to be the creative genius that God had called me to be. She and Dr. Black were my Pushers.

Marta allowed me to be me, unapologetically. She was very *"woke"* to the struggles of Black and Brown people of color.

At first glance some may have thought she was white, but her long semi-thick black hair would make you ponder and think that maybe she was mixed with Native American. And you would be wrong, She is Hispanic of Mexican descent.

I loved to hear her tell stories about her parents. She taught me how to tell stories, how to be a person of integrity, and how to engage in ethical behavior as a competitor and a coach. She always went by the rules, and she never showed any favorites. She encouraged us to take topics that we were passionate about. Under her leadership, our team went to national contests for the first time in 27 years.

Marta took us to see a play in California titled, "Nigger, Wetback, Chink (NWC)." This play looked at the stereotypical roles three young men were cast into and gave them a platform to educate their audiences. The play creates a dialog to have safe conversations about race, culture, and stereotypes while challenging systemic racism.

I was like a leaf shaking in the wind when I started attending ECC and joined the speech team. Dr. Shadwell gave me permission to embrace my 6'1, 400-pound size. She encouraged me to own any room where I dared to speak or walk into. She taught me to always be bold, confident, informative, passionate, engaging, persuasive, entertaining, and above all, to have fun. She always gave the best speeches to entertain. She changed my life that day and I've never forgotten that conversation we had.

When I come across someone experiencing the same internal struggle, I share with them the same pearls of wisdom that Dr. Gail Shadwell gave me. I simply give them permission to release the greatness inside themselves.

Pushers go by many different names or titles in life. Midwives, mentors, counselors, and coaches all can help you give birth to your purpose and destiny.

As I began to prepare for my studies at Spelman, I researched the requirements and spoke to some of the staff on campus. It was then that I met one of the most amazing women, Mrs. Moon, who was the assistant registrar. Sweet, smart, and encouraging, she was my Spelman Pusher.

Every time she picked up the phone to take my call, she inspired me to continue to pursue my dream of attending Spelman. She always reminded me,

"Tanell, you have this. You can do it."

She encouraged me to have faith in God and in myself. When I finally met her in person, she looked just like I had imagined. Short, petite, and light-skinned, with a head full of dark brown hair. She had a smile that invited you in like your grandma's comfort food. When I arrived at Spelman and met her, I knew I was in good hands.

Pearls of Wisdom

I Am Your Pusher

- Everyone needs a *Pusher* to live out their purpose.

- Your Pusher may not even look like you, like you, be your friend, be friendly towards you, or have much in common with you.

- Your Pusher will help you evolve, matriculate, and metamorphose into who you are called to be.

- Some Pushers are seasonal; be willing to let them go so they can move on to their next assignment.

- Never hoard greatness. It is meant to be shared.

- Be sure to pay forward the lessons and the pearls of wisdom that were given to you by your Pushers.

- Respect your Pusher's time and value their worth.

- Foster excellent communication with your Pushers and learn all that they are willing to teach.

- Gracefully seize opportunities to become others' Pushers and motivators.

- You have to be teachable, respectful, open to change, and susceptible to correcting.

- A great Pushers will know how to build you up without destroying your self-efficacy.

- When working with your Pushers don't allow the spirit offense to stop you from receiving from your Pushers.
- Get out of your feelings and out of your own way.

Chapter 9

The Hardest Thing

> *The hard part of life is we have to keep on living even when our world has stopped spinning, and all the stars are laying at our feet.*
>
> —Sayinggoodbye.org

Death never asks, "Is this a good time for me to turn your world upside down, and your life inside out?" Death just happens regardless if you are ready or not. I definitely was not ready for my youngest brother Jeremey's life to be snuffed out. Jojo Moyes, captured my raw emotions in this quote: "Losing him was like having a hole shot straight through me, a painful, constant reminder, an absence I could never fill."

Jeremey was such a free spirit. He was the definition of fearless to me. He grabbed life by the horns and rode it as far as it would take him. And he was one of the funniest people I have ever known.

He walked slightly on his tippy toes and had a slight stutter that only made cameos when he had a sudden burst of emotion.

To this day my sister Nada believes that the media killed our brother. My brother was killed not because of what he did, but because of what he knew.

Jeremy could not go anywhere without his picture being flashed across the television: *Jeremy Henry, wanted for questioning, in connection with a double murder.*

I was later told by my sister that our brother warned the guys who committed the murder that they had better do something to clear his name by a certain day... *or he would.*

The double murder of a white teenager and an Asian teenager occurred not too far from the small, quiet, sleepy town where I grew up. You could the racial tension and grief hanging in the air. I often wondered if the police and media would have cared, or responded the same way if it was the double murder of two Black teenage boys.

I was devastated by the loss of my brother. I later found out that my brother's killer was paid $1,000 and given a necklace. I could not fathom how someone could calculate the value of another human being's life that way. My family knew that whoever killed my brother was someone he knew and trusted. My brother never went anywhere without his gun and never allowed anyone to walk up to him.

My brother was shot multiple times from behind with a handgun. When he took his last breath, I woke up out of my sleep. I knew something was wrong. I began to pray and ask God to show me what was wrong, then eventually went back to sleep.

The next morning, while getting ready for church, my sister called me and asked, "Nell, where are you at?" She spoke slowly and hesitantly. As if she was choosing how to spoon-feed me each word. I told her I was at Kyle's house getting ready for church. I had recently become homeless due to me being a struggling college student and not budgeting well what little money I had. My friend Kyle and her family allowed me to move in with them. She'd said to me,

"Mocha, I spoke to my husband and cannot bear you moving into that little roach-infested apartment. We have a full basemenbbt that is not finished yet, but you are welcome to it. There is a pull-out sofa down there that you can sleep on to get yourself together. We would love to have you here with us."

Looking at her you would never have guessed we were friends. She was White, middle-aged, and married with kids. We had met on the speech team, and we simply adored our friendship. We helped each other through some of our most difficult times in life. About a year prior to me being evicted Kyle received some devastating news. "Mocha, I went to the doctor, and he said they have to do a biopsy. They are saying I may have cancer. Mocha, what about my kids…"

I listened to my friend, but then I began to quiet her fears. I responded, "Kyle, let's pray!"

She did in fact have cancer. As a friend and a hairstylist, I was honored when I saw her two weeks later. "Mocha I am going to do more than survive this." With sheer determination in her eyes, Kyle asked, "Mocha the chemo is going to take out all my hair. Can you cut it short?"

I knew what Kyle was saying without saying it. She was letting cancer know that if was going to take her hair out, it was going to be on her own terms.

After draping Kyle, I pulled my sterling silver shears out of their case. As I began to cut her soft, light brown hair, one tear slid down her cheek as we sat quietly embarking on her journey of transformation, healing, and wholeness for a brief moment. Then as girlfriends do, we started talking and laughing. When I had finished, I gave her a hand-held mirror to check out her new look.

I gave her a minute to grieve the loss of her hair by herself before I came in. As she checked herself out her eyes widened and she declared, "Oh Mocha, I love it. Thank you!"

Kyle fought her fight against cancer bravely and won. There were days she cried and was filled with uncertainty and pain, but she refused to give up. It was her love for God and family that pushed her along when she wanted to quit.

"At Kyle's!"

I answered in an upbeat and positive voice. She said, "Early this morning they found Jeremy dead." Her voice began to crack slightly from the trauma and sorrow she was holding in to deliver this gut-wrenching blow to my heart. There is nothing that can prepare you for the news of a loved one's sudden death.

I will never forget the pain and anguish I saw in my brother Henry's eyes. My sister still struggles to eat pancakes and red velvet cake because he made the best pancakes, and he loved red velvet cake.

I found myself angry at God for not showing me this as a prophet. I felt that if I had known it would happen, I could have done something to warn him, or to save him. I did not understand how God showed me things about strangers and random people but had hidden this from me.

In my anger with God, I became a very combative person. Jeremy's death gave me a front-row seat to how cruel and evil human beings can be to one another.

I never allowed myself to stay angry at Jeremy's killer. I knew that him getting the death penalty or spending the rest of his natural life in prison was not going to bring my brother back. Not sure why, but it was easy for me to forgive my brother's killer. Maybe it's because I am a

Christian, or maybe it's because I wanted someone to exercise the same grace and forgiveness toward my brother.

As I sat in church during our 10:30 a.m. worship service, I felt a gentle warm hand on my shoulder. I turned slightly and saw it was my Pastor. After he prayed for me, we agreed that I was going home to bury my brother and minister to my family, not to grieve the loss of my brother, yet. We both knew God was up to something. I flew to Florida from Chicago, knowing that I would grieve the death of my brother when I got back home.

There are days that I still lament the loss of both of my brothers. Jeremey died before I made it to Spelman, and my older brother Henry died after I had finished graduate school. Learning to live without my brothers is the hardest thing I have had to do in my life. Yet their lives and premature deaths inspire me to live my life to the fullest.

Every day, I am going to live life like it is an adventure, because tomorrow is not promised to anyone.

My brothers no longer have the gift of life, and this truth forces me to beat back the shadows of heaviness and clouds of depression that sometimes hover over me.

Some days I have to remind myself, *Those we love don't go away, they walk beside us every day...unseen, unheard, but always near, still loved, still missed and very dear.* (https://quotesbae.com/).

The reality is that, although my brothers are gone, they will never be forgotten. I will forever cherish our memories and make sure their legacies live on through their children.

Jeremy and Henry, the hardest thing I have had to do is find the courage and willpower to be brave enough to live my life without the two of you.

Pearls of Wisdom

The Hardest Thing

- The loss of a loved one is never an easy thing to get over. Give yourself time to celebrate their life and grieve their loss.

- Never ask a person who has just lost a loved one how they are doing. Instead, ask them how they are doing today. Each day is different, so asking about that day helps them take things one day at a time.

- Never bombard them with questions pertaining to the death of their loved one who died suddenly; it could be traumatic and overwhelming.

- Everyone grieves the loss of a loved one differently. Do not try to help the person based on what you think is best for them. Help them based on what is best for them, who they are, and what they need.

- Always seek grief counseling and pastoral care after the death of a loved one.

Chapter 10

My Math is Bad: Two Years = Four Years

> *"If [it, or] they are not adding to you, then you need to do the subtracting."*
>
> —Bishop Carlton Winfrey

Never allow anyone or anything to waste your time. I say this often since I learned it: "Time is the number one dream thief." Do not allow anyone to pass you through the system. If you do not know enough to go to the next level, then stay at the current level and get the knowledge you will need to succeed at the next level.

We have a negative perception of students being held back, failing, or having to repeat a course, and that should never be the case. This creates a performance-based learning system. In such a system, learning for knowledge and education are not the objectives; rather, high enough grades to pass to the next level is the objective. Yes, we want to pass and matriculate to the next level, but if we are not learning we are fostering a **diploma-mill kind** of learning rather than one based on merit.

My mother, who is not college-educated, is one of the smartest people I have ever met. She is naturally gifted with wisdom and intellect that were not taught to her in a school setting.

Historically, some people of color did not have the highest level of education, but many of them had the basic skills they needed such as arithmetic, reading, writing, and life skills to be successful and to become gainfully employed.

Do not misunderstand what I am saying, I believe in the importance of education, but I also believe in the importance of life skills. There are some people who may not be exceptional students according to traditional learning standards, but they may be geniuses in the very thing they were created to do.

My math was bad because I had advisors in college who did not care enough about me to help me formulate a successful plan to spend only two years at ECC. They only did enough to say they had done their job. No one took the time to walk me through what it would take for me to graduate in two years. I was just picking classes that were open and available until I learned there were certain classes I had to take to earn my Associate Arts Degree.

In fact, I remember someone telling me, "I don't know why, but Black people do not finish at ECC." I was determined to matriculate after hearing that. I would learn how to be my own best advocate and not sit in another advisor's office and let them dictate what classes I was going to take. I'd had enough of this "Children of Israel" experience of wandering around in the wilderness for 40 years. It was time for me to go to the next level.

I began to sense that people had negative thoughts and opinions about me being at ECC for so long. I was currently in my fourth year of attending ECC year-round. No one ever asked or really cared why I had been there so long. I went through a lot while pursuing my dream of making it to Spelman College.

I had to learn how to be a college student with a learning disability, to deal with family drama and the murder of my brother, and at times to be homeless.

One day, while walking through the halls of the main lobby, a White teacher looked at me intently and lovingly and asked, "When are you graduating?"

I replied, "I am graduating this year."

"Good!" she replied. "Leave this place and go explore other institutions. You have been here long enough. It's time to spread your wings."

I smiled politely and laughed it off. Aware that what I had been discerning was true.

I knew it was time for me to go. Destiny was calling me, and I had no more time to spend at this academic level. I knew that I was going to Spelman even if I had to kick the door down, as I have often told people.

My Auntie Jewel used to tell me, "Niece, I see you there." Anytime I got discouraged, she reminded me of my purpose. For almost four years, I took and retook classes at ECC to earn my associate degree.

Pearls of wisdom

My Math is Bad: Two Years = Four Years

➤ You can't rush greatness, but you can actively nurture it.

➤ Do not allow yourself to wander through life without a plan of completion for each goal that you set.

➤ Use the SMART system when it comes to setting goals for yourself and sticking to them. You must be *specific* about the details of your goals and how you will obtain them, as well as some of the obstacles and challenges you will face. This is also the who, what, why, when, and how of the process. These are the essential details needed to help you reach your goals. You must set *measurable* goals that you can track. This will help you do a better self-inventory of your strengths, weaknesses, and progress. Make sure you set *achievable* goals. This can be a struggle for some people who are creative geniuses, because in their minds, regardless of how big or small the goal is, it is obtainable. This is also very true for people who live their lives based on faith. This brings me to my next point, which is that we have to set *reasonable and realistic* goals so that we are not all over the place.

➤ Our true and divine goals that align with our purpose may appear unrealistic, but with God, all things are possible. And lastly, there is *time*. Timing is everything. We all have heard the cliché,

➤ Time waits for no one. Two of the greatest lessons I have learned about time are:

- Time is the number one dream thief, and Time is neither negative nor positive; it is neutral.
- You need an accountability partner who will hold you accountable.
- An academic coach for students with a learning disability is a must.
- Find what inspires you to be the best version of yourself and use it as your muse.
- Always do a self-inventory of tasks and goals that you are struggling to complete.
- Ask yourself, *Why am I struggling to complete this task and what can I do better or more quickly to complete this task?*
- Be honest with yourself when you drop the ball.

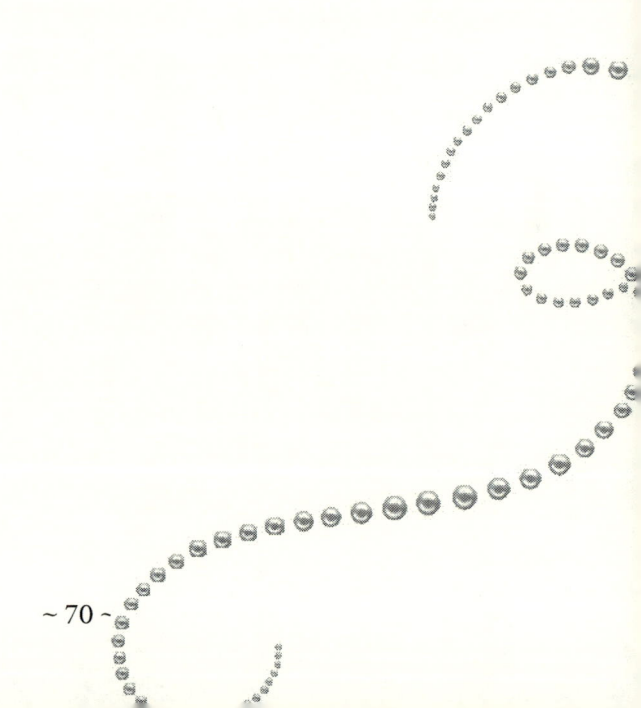

Chapter 11

Kicking Down Doors

> "You can't knock on an opportunity's door and not be ready."
>
> —Bruno Mars

I knew by faith that I was going to Spelman College, even if I had to kick down the door to get in. Failure was not an option. No matter what I had to go through, I was going to make it. I had made up my mind that nothing would stop me from reaching my goal, because I was unstoppable through Christ Jesus.

I knew by faith that I had stood and "fought the good fight by faith." And I knew that anyone or anything standing in the way or speaking against my vision, my purpose, my destiny, was not for me. In fact, I view them as my adversaries, even if they happen to be my family, spouse, friend, or child. In Hebrew the word for Satan is *Hasata*, which translates as *adversary*. If someone does not believe in you and does not encourage you to be the best divine and authentic version of yourself, then they are not for you.

You have to tell yourself— regardless of who or what they are— they are your adversaries, and a distraction from your purpose. You can see in certain parts of Jesus' ministry where others tried to use his familiar relationships against him. There will always be someone in the crowd who will come along to cause confusion and distract you from your purpose through familiar bonds and relationships.

In the book of Matthew 12:46–50, the passage illustrates that while Jesus was engaging in ministry, his mother and brother came up to the front of the crowd.

The people began to talk amongst themselves, *"Yo' momma and little brother just rolled up and they don't want to talk to you."* Jesus then asked, *"Who is my momma and brother? He pointed to his disciples and said, Yo, look this is my brother, sister, and mother, those who are doing the will of my Father in heaven."*

Some of the people who were standing and sitting around them had the sole purpose of being spectators, to stir up confusion. Yet Jesus' family understood that this was his time to focus and do what He was called to do. Jesus' mentality was, *I am willing to knock on the door politely, but I am prepared to deal with anything or anyone that tries to derail the will and the purpose of God.*

Throughout my life I had to learn that anyone or anything that stands in the way of my goals, dreams, and purpose is my adversary. There have been many times when I have needed tunnel vision and focus on things that helped me fulfill my purpose, as opposed to doing things my family and friends would have preferred. I had to sacrifice time and some experiences to hone the greatness inside of me unapologetically.

Pearls of Wisdom

Kicking Down Doors

- Sometimes you have to selfish in order to hone the greatness inside of you.
- Your adversary is anyone who gets in the way of your purpose.
- Kicking down doors ain't easy, but it requires strong legs and courage in the face of adversity.
- Failure is not an option when you are mastering your purpose, it is just a learning experience.
- Kicking down doors requires one to have faith.
- Make your mind up and stick to whatever your goals and dreams are.
- Don't allow dream killers to stop you from kicking down doors of opposition to your purpose.
- Never be afraid to create innovative doors that provide opportunities to give life and feed your purpose.

Chapter 12

Not Everyone is Going to be Happy for You

> *They're gonna try to tell you no, shatter all your dreams. But you gotta get up and go and think better things.*
>
> —Mac Miller

Being accepted into Spelman College was one of the most amazing things that has ever happened in my life. I worked hard to earn my acceptance letter to become a part of the Spelman legacy. God told me I was going to Spelman. I knew I was getting in. I was going to get accepted based on all of my hard work and determination, or I was going to kick the door down to get in. I was going to work hard regardless of anyone or anything that got in my way of pursuing my purpose

I knew that going to and graduating from Spelman was more than just a silly dream to me. It was a part of my destiny and purpose. And although God had told me I was going, I still had to put in the work to fulfill God's best for my life. I knew that if I did not get in, then it was not because this was not part of my purpose, but because I had not done my part in positioning myself to be accepted.

I began to look into what was needed to be accepted into Spelman. I remember sitting in the computer lab at ECC and trying to do my research. The first thing I realized was that I did not know how to spell Spelman. In frustration, I began to cry. As hot, moist tears fell from my eyes, I told myself, *You are going to be ok.*

Remember the first time you came to this lab? You cried because you sat here twenty minutes embarrassed that you did not know how to turn the computer on? Now look at you. You just earned a B in your first computer class and made your first website. You can do anything.

I started laughing, saying to myself, "I can do anything but spell." Spelman must have the word spell and men in it since that's how it sounds. As I looked up how to spell Spelman College, I reminded myself, *I can do this. I can spell it. I can and I will get accepted into Spelman College.* Even though my heart was still heavy and my spirit low, from not knowing how to spell Spelman. I made myself study the spelling of the next chapter of my life: S-P-E-L-M-A-N College.

I often visited the website to make sure I was staying the course of what was needed to apply and be accepted. I also took time to see where some well-known alums of Spelman had ended up, to draw inspiration from them. I learned that Spelman Women excelled and have made history in various arenas. I was totally blown away when I learned Alice Walker, Keisha Knight Pulliam, Esther Rolle, Dr. Bernice King, Adrienne-Joi Johnson, Stayce Adams, Rolonda Watts, Andrea Nicole Livingstone, Linda Goode Bryant, Namina Forna, Spike Trotman, Clara Ann Howard, Emma Beard Delaney, Monica Mongomery, Lashanda Holmes, Blanch Armwood, Marion Wright Edelman, and LaTanya Richardson Jackson are my Spelman Sisters. These women inspired because each one of them reflected something I loved, a gift I had, or part of my purpose.

I occasionally took time to call the admissions office and became close with the assistant registrar Mrs. Moon, who was always so helpful and inspiring. I knew that God had given her that job just for me. Her voice always encouraged me to keep fighting even when everything in me wanted to give up.

I remember walking down the hallway one day at ECC and just needing a little motivation. I called Spelman with a question, and just like that, my motivation to excel and to accomplish my dream of transferring to Spelman was back.

Mrs. Moon, encouraged me, *"Tanell you have to hang in there! You can do this. God has a plan for you, but you cannot quit on the plan."*

I knew she was right, but I was so tired of working hard and going to school year-round. She always knew the right thing to say to me to inspire me to take another step, by faith.

Not getting accepted into Spelman was never an option for me. Yet, I was starting to get anxious because it was weeks past the admissions notification deadline and I still didn't receive my acceptance letter. I remember scanning through the checklist that I had memorized in my head. I remember thinking like, *Wow, I hope my college essay was good enough, that I did not have to take the ACT. I reminded myself "I have 90 credit hours, I am transferring in with an associate degree. I have a 3.4 GPA and excellent letters of recommendation."* I called to mind what my Auntie Jewel had prophesied to me, "I see you there, niece."

I began to pray and talk to My Heavenly Father. *God, what's good? You told me I was going.*

God, I have been through hell and high water to accomplish this dream and fulfill my destiny and purpose. For four years, God, I have gone to school year-round, penniless, working multiple jobs, through family drama, homelessness, the death of Jeremy, taking intermediate math 096 and 098 four times each before passing with a C. I devoted my entire summer to taking statistics just so I can walk into Spelman with an Associate of Arts Degree and have all my credits accepted.

God, I need you to help me with this one solid because you told me I was going to Spelman, and I did the work that was required of me. Father God, now I need your favor to open the door for me.

As I called to check the status of my application, I tried to remain upbeat and positive. My voice was trembling slightly as I inquired.

"Hello, my name is Tanell Vashawn Allen. I applied to Spelman College but I never received a letter notification to inform me if I was accepted, or denied. Can you please see if I was accepted?"

She said, "You did not get a letter yet? Then you didn't get in. Wait, let me check. Tell me your full name again and your mailing address?"

"My name is Tanell Vashawn Allen. My address is 104 Woodland Court Apt 4, Carpentersville, IL 60110."

"Give me one minute please!"

It seemed like the longest and loudest moment **ever.** I could hear my heart beating violently in my chest. When the lady on the other end of the phone returned, she told me, *"Yes, you got accepted!"*

"Yessss! I knew it!"

She replied, *"Congratulations, Ms. Allen. Welcome to Spelman. I will resend your acceptance letter to your address."*

When I found out I was officially accepted to Spelman, I felt like doing a victory lap around my office, but my better judgment kicked in. I worked in a records and registration office. I don't think my boss would have minded at all; they probably would have started running with me. They were super supportive of my goals and dreams.

I could not wait to share this news with the people most important to me. My core tribe of friends were so excited for me, especially Auntie Jewel. I remember singing to her, "I got good news, Auntie."

She said, "What, you got into Spelman!"

A huge smile came across my face. "Yep!"

My auntie just got me. I always loved hanging out with her, shopping late at night, and sleeping in bed with her.

"That's a good niece. I am so proud of you."

"Thank you, Auntie! Man, God is so good! I have worked so hard and long to get into Spelman.

I have gone to Elgin Community College for four years, year-round, Auntie, and to finally see my dream come to fruition is something I cannot even express in words."

When I told my mother, it was not a big deal verbally.

"Momma I got accepted to Spelman College!"

I held my breath, for a few seconds waiting for my mother to say something. Even though I knew my mother was proud of me, she never made a big fuss over my successes or accomplishments in front of me, although I knew she bragged on me to others

She replied, "Mmmhmm, that's good. I don't know much about Spelman other than what I saw on the Cosby Show. I am going to tell you this, don't think everybody is going to be happy for you because you got accepted to Spelman."

It was as if someone had just deflated me.

She continued, "You are going to have to work extra hard now that you got accepted into Spelman. You have to be on time. Do you understand me, Tanell? Everybody is not going to be excited for you or going to help you. You can do this. It is time for you to step your game up."

If anybody else had heard this, they would have been heartbroken. But not me. My mother is a very black-or-white person. There is no gray area. All my life she has encouraged and pushed me to be greatness in motion. She knows how to be brutally honest with me to foster true creativity and growth.

I tucked in her words of wisdom. It was humbling for me not to allow my accomplishments to go to my head, but to continue to raise the momentum of excellence without the permission or approval of others. In these pearls of wisdom my mother was forewarning that there were going to be people who will not congratulate me or assist me with my journey to higher education. She gave me a stern dose of a reality I had to learn to be OK with.

This prepared me to stay focused, to be invested in my goals and dreams.

It also inspired me to work even harder to ensure that I graduated from Spelman because getting in was the easy part. Now I had to push myself to graduate on time.

Pearls of Wisdom

Not Everybody Is Going to be Happy for You

- Do not try to please everyone. Being a people pleaser will leave you frustrated and irritated at the end of the day.
- Learn to be in the room and not always have to be the center of attention in the room.
- Do not share your goals and dreams with people who do not believe, support, and affirm the greatness in you.
- Learn to move with purpose in silence.
- You must make necessary sacrifices to protect your dream from dream-killers.
- Sometimes honesty can be your best motivation.
- Never allow the spirit of offense to stop you from receiving sound wisdom and instructions.
- Wisdom always comes from a place of love and understanding.
- As Katt Williams says "If you ain't got no haters, you ain't doing something right."

Chapter 13

"Can You Wear White, Young Lady?"

> *"And on the 11th day of April, God gave man the greatest gift of all: The Spelman woman."*
>
> —*Unknown*

Well, can you? If you've ever seen the movie *The Nutty Professor,* you may remember this line from Sherman Klump's grandmother, played by multi-talented Eddie Murphy. Everyone loved Sherman's sexually aware and outspoken grandmother. Everybody is familiar with this running joke that has made cameos, on the chitlin' circuit, on the silver screen, as well as on television. This simple question is very loaded and pertains to women's rights, their sexuality, and their bodies. I have never heard anyone playfully ask, "Can you wear white, young man?"

This simple phrase almost ruined my entire pre-Spelman experience, and it had nothing to do with sexual purity.

The White Dress Ceremony is a huge part of Spelman College's tradition. It is to be followed with respect, honor, and dignity as we pay homage to our founders who paved the way for us. During this ceremony you are to wear a white dress, flesh-tone stockings, black dress shoes, and the only jewelry you can wear is a watch.

I had worked hard to accomplish my dream of attending Spelman College and I was not about to let not one thing stop me from experiencing every aspect of my dream.

My size almost ruined my White Dress Ceremony. I wanted to share this experience with the women in my family. My sister and my mother were always so great at helping me find the right outfit and shoes to fit my massive body.

I wanted shopping for my white dress to be a beautiful bonding experience with my grandmother, my mother, my sister and me, but it turned out to be a major nightmare, worse than on Elm Street.

I do not know who was getting more irritated, me or my mother. My sister Nada was "cool in the game." After we visited what had to be like the seventh store, my mother suggested, "Nell, maybe you can get a nice white skirt and shirt and wear that because we are going through hell trying to find a white dress to fit you." I stubbornly cried and shook my head, angrily answering, "No! I am going to have a white dress like everybody else. You have to wear a white dress."

What was wrong with my Momma? Was she crazy? All the work, all of the sacrifices I had made to live out my dream of attending Spelman College would be in vain, if I gave up on finding a white dress. The White Dress Ceremony was an essential part of my Spelman College experience. I was not going to settle for wearing **no damn** white skirt and shirt just because it is hard to find one simple white dress to fit my plus-size body.

I was willing to pay up to $500 for the dress. My mother's comments made me anxious and irritated. I was overlooking a dress out of the fear of her being right. Maybe there was no white dress big enough to fit me. What if I did have to wear flip-flops, a white tee-shirt, and a skirt to the White Dress Ceremony?

Finally, we stopped at Catherine's in Tampa, and I found a white dress that not only fit but flattered my large body. To my surprise and delight, the dress was only $100.00

"This is it! This is my white dress!" I celebrated.

This symbolic ceremony is reflective of what our founders had envisioned, which was their best.

Oh, don'cha you wish you were a Spelmanite!
Oh, don'cha wish you were a Spelmanite! We're the oh so fine divas of AUC!

I was ready for my big day! I arrived on campus early to make sure I could get ready in the dorms with my Spelman Sisters. I got ready in the Morehouse James Dorm. I was feeling confident until I began to see more and more of my Spelman Sisters in their white dresses. Then I began to play the comparison game.

I am older than most of these girls! I am bigger than them! She is darker than I am! I don't look like the image of the Spelman Woman! I have a learning disability I am probably not nearly as smart as these girls.
They probably got a full ride whereas I am taking out student loans. Look at their shoes! Their feet are so small. My feet are huge. I have large feet. At least I have a prettier face than some of these girls.

Although I was silently comparing and measuring myself against each of my sisters, I inwardly told myself, *I am worthy enough to be here. Who I am is enough. I worked hard to be here just like every one of my sisters did.*

I guess I should have been paying closer attention to where I was walking as I left the dorm, because before I knew what was going on, I stepped down onto a bad crack in the sidewalk and broke the heel of my right shoe. "SHIT!" Whelp— there goes all my fancy French Man! God, you have got to be kidding me! *Yo*, I ***cannot*** handle this ***today*****!"**

I felt the tears swelling up inside of me and I knew I was on the verge of having a meltdown. After I cried about my life going to hell in a handbasket and how un-perfect it all was, I dried my eyes and told myself, *Who I am is enough. I deserve to be here.* After my mini breakdown, I limped over to line up with my Spelman Sisters outside on the oval across from Morehouse James dorms. I gazed at the arch and the beautiful, lush patches of grass that the oval outlined.

As I stood there my mood began to lighten. I cannot fully describe the feeling of awe that came over me as I walked in line next to my Spelman Sister, as we walked towards Sisters Chapel in pairs of two. It was something about this moment that was life changing.

I was excited to be on the campus of Spelman College. During the first week of freshman orientation, we were asked to wear skirts so that we could easily be identified as new *Spelmanites*. This was the first time I had ever wanted to wear a skirt without any hesitation. I often shied away from wearing skirts and dresses because I always felt that I had "a body that was made wrong." The best way to describe my body at that time was shaped like a trapezoid or like the cartoon character Johnny Bravo, yet it has changed drastically now.

My younger brother Jeremy used to say, "You shaped up there like an ironing board." He would also say, "Nell, you suffer from that disease no-ass-at-all," and would even call me, "Flap-a-jack-no-ass-in-the-back." Jeremy poking fun at me never bothered me. I always knew he was joking, but if someone else had said those very same things to me, there was a strong possibility that they would end up in the hospital in critical condition, or dead. He was a force to be reckoned with. He was the youngest, but he was protective of his loved ones, especially his siblings.

I guess I did not fit what some deemed to be the "image of a Spelman Woman," but no one could deny that I was pretty. I'd secretly always wanted to be a plus-size model since the age of fourteen. I heard one of my older Spelman Sisters, who worked at the college as a security guard, say, "You used to have to submit Polaroid pictures of yourself in the 1980s when you applied."

Most people have a preconceived notion of what a *Spelmanite* is. They picture her as being educated, sophisticated, well-polished, groomed, articulate, skinny, cake-faced, wearing pearls, and at times bourgeoisie. Some of these stereotypes are true, some aren't. However, these stereotypes could be true or false at any all-female higher learning institution, not just Spelman.

While I can honestly say that I did not fit into the stereotypical image of a *Spelmanite,* neither did many of my amazing Spelman Sisters. Some of us were plus-size, thin, athletic, average build, tall, and short. Some of our hair were natural, locs, permed, curly, or pressed. We were creatives, intellectuals, and more.

We were and are the Baskin-Robbins of Spelmanites. We were simple women ready to change the world in our own way by becoming part of a legacy of greatness. Many of us were the first in our families to attend Spelman College, yet because of our experiences, we will not be the last.

This is why we must debunk these stereotypical images of what a Spelman woman looks like. She looks like you and me. It is imperative that we continue to hold the door open for more generations of women of color so we can proudly say, "May her first steps be towards Spelman."

Pearls of Wisdom

"Can You Wear White Young Lady?"

- ➢ Never give up on your dreams regardless of how long it takes to achieve them.

- ➢ Never allow other people's opinions to cloud your vision.

- ➢ You have to tell yourself, "I am not supposed to fit in when God created me to be the standard."

- ➢ You are "The apple of God's eye."

- ➢ "You are beautiful and fearfully made."

- ➢ Always see yourself based on what the Bible says, "You are 'your own kind of beautiful.'"

- ➢ Be willing to go the extra mile and invest in yourself, because you are worth it.

- ➢ Make sure your standards of beauty reflect the glory of God and your core values and not what the media and mainstream society dictate.

Chapter 14

Living My Dream

> *Dreams do come true if you believe.*
> —Walt Disney

In the days and weeks leading up to me leaving for Spelman, it was getting harder and harder for me to sit through church service on Sundays. One week I sat there silently, saying to myself, *Next Sunday is my last Sunday here*, and sighing with relief. I was fully ready to move to Atlanta University City (AUC), the consortium that includes Spelman. My co-workers at ECC had thrown me a going away party where they all had given me gift cards to furnish my dorm room. I sat there thinking, *Man, I am so ready to go...*, when my Pastor started doing this warm announcement/invitation for the congregation to bless me.

"Our very own Sister Tanell, some of you know her by Mocha, will be leaving us next Sunday. She is leaving for Atlanta, GA where she will be attending Spelman College. She has been serving here for the last three years. Many of you are here because of her. She works with youth, is a part of the evangelism team, and volunteers at Elgin Soup kitchen...."

I had been briefly resting my eyes. Everything in me was in countdown mode. My eyes shot open with shock. I'd known they were going to bless me, but I was really surprised by the extent they went to. All the children from the youth ministry came pouring out with these beautiful cards that they had made for me.

My pastors, who were like my parents, gifted me with a nice leather bag/briefcase to carry some of my school supplies. I was ready to "run on to see what my end was going to be."

The church also helped me financially, and the congregation blessed me. I received the Sallie Mae "Achieving Your Dreams Scholarship," as well as a scholarship from ECC's TRiO Department. More students need to utilize the resources that TRiO offers to aid them in successfully completing their academic goals. I do not know if I would have graduated without the much-needed tools and assistance they provided. Years later, I received my first paid speaking engagement from ECC's TRiO department.

Bam-Bam-Bam! *Suuugaaa-Hon-naaay-Iccce-teee!*
My mind was screeching as I thought, WHO THE HELL IS KNOCKING LIKE THE POLICE? I was so shocked when I opened the door and saw Pastor Faith, co-pastor at my church, was standing at our door. Neisy, Dontae, and I overslept. Neisy and I were college roommates. Dontae was one of the youths who was a part of the youth department and really took a liking to me and Neisy. Weeks before I went away to college he practically lived at our house.

We welcomed him with open arms. He was well-mannered and funny, and a joy to be around. This kid pulled on my heartstrings.

We quickly got ready and rushed to O'Hare Airport. This was my official last day living in Carpentersville, Illinois.

I was nervous and excited at the same time. I was flying home to Dade City, Florida, first, then Nada was going to drive me there and make sure I got set up. My sister Granada (aka Nada) would take you out of this world to defend one of her siblings. She has always been a mother figure and overprotective of us. I cannot think of anyone else more deserving of accompanying me on this rite of passage. My big sister was honored to drive me to college. Anybody else would have driven too slowly. My dream had been deferred for over ten years and I was ready to fully live and experience it.

At the mature age of twenty-eight. I could not believe I was finally living my dream of attending Spelman. Tyler Perry tells us, "Tyler Perry studio is a place where dreams do come true." Wow, I can say the same thing about Spelman College. It was more than I ever dreamed it would be. Olive Branch, an AUC first-year student tradition, was amazing. Behold a sea of Black pride, brilliance, and unity as Spelman, Morehouse, and Clark Atlanta students came together to celebrate and welcome the incoming class of students. We walked, sweated, and cheered together as we embraced the beginning of our new journey.

I was slightly embarrassed to be 28 years old and going to school with 17 and 18-year-old young ladies. It took me a while to get over it.

One of my younger Spelman Sisters called me Ms. Tanell. *Just pour the oldness on now*, I thought. Although I looked young, I was a natural leader and a motherly figure. They were my tell-tells that I was much older than many of my classmates. These skill sets were divinely given to me, but they have been fostered and sharpened with experience, love, and time.

I slowly got over this as I met more and more Pauline Drake Scholars, who were older students who decided to attend Spelman later in life. Some of them were even transfer students. They had decided to fight against the odds of achieving their dreams too. Many of them had kids, were married, divorced, in their second career, pastors, working for Spelman, had previously held corporate jobs, or lost children and spouses. One even fought *cancer* and WON, but *never lost her hair.*

I loved the fact that I was able to wake up every day and live out my dream of attending Spelman College. I found myself in love with the culture of the AUC and the Black excellence that was all around me. I was honored that my smother-mother of a sister drove me to college. It has literally always been her against the world for us.

As we pulled up to Spelman's campus we were greeted by the orientation committee and given directions to follow.

The energy on campus was warm, welcoming, and exciting. As my sister and I mingled among the students, my sister's face beamed with pride and honor. I knew she was proud of me. As we went through the cafeteria line, she stood there looking odd at first, then confessed to me, "I wish I had gone to college." The look on her face was a look of remorse. I wonder how different my sister's life would have been had she had the same opportunities I did in life. She suffered a lot of abuse and hardships so Jeremy, Henry, and I did not have to. She endured the brunt of my mother's behavior due to her addiction.

I remember my sister lying about her age at thirteen in order to get a summer job that required her to be fourteen. She has always made sacrifices to make sure her loved ones had what they needed. Even at 28 and away at college, my sister always paid my phone bill and bought me school clothes and plane tickets.

My sister and I were both surprised to find out that I was on the waiting list for housing at Spelman. I thought I was going to lose it in all that Georgia heat. "What do you mean I am on the waiting list for housing? I paid my deposit." I said, with a slight attitude. I could feel the warm hot tears threatening to escape. I knew that if I allowed just one tear to fall, there would be nothing but waterworks. My sister could feel my frustration and quickly took over the conversation.

We were told because I was a transfer student housing was not guaranteed for me until after all the traditional students had housing. "What?" I questioned angrily. "Why didn't you guys tell me this prior to me arriving? I paid a dorm deposit to have a room. Now you are telling me I am about to be homeless. This is unacceptable." I tried to not be the good ole cutup, but I am about to snap Chicago-style. I feel my inner South-Side chick about to come out.

An employee stepped up and quickly assured me that I would not be homeless, and that Spelman had many resources for housing for their transfer students who commuted back and forth to campus within the neighborhood. In the commuter office I was given some resources for housing within walking distance of campus.

When I got back into my sister's big blue suburban, I let all of my frustration out through silent tears mixed with sweat.

Damn! I was sweating cats and dogs in this Georgia heat. They were not lying when they deemed this the Hot *Lanta.*

I felt robbed of my Spelman experience. I had wanted to live on campus so I could have the dorm and campus life experiences that I grew up watching on *A Different World.*

My sister assured me that she would not leave until we found adequate, safe, and affordable housing for me near campus. She was a gentle cool breeze on that hot, sticky, and frustrating day. We visited about three houses that had rooms for rent before I found a place that I loved. It was down the hill from Morehouse's Perdue Hall Dorms. I loved the fact that if I walked up the hill and through the gates I would be on Morehouse's Campus. Say what you wanna, "I am single and ready to mingle."

The young lady who showed us the house was nice, polite, and professional. She operated in the role of the manager and big sister of the house. Her name in the Bible means beginning and end. I took this as a sign from God that this was where He wanted me to have my beautiful new beginning. *Al* reminded me of a mixture of the characters Kim and Jalisa from *A Different World*. I don't usually get star-struck, but I was impressed and inspired to be living in the house with a Black woman who was making a name for herself in the television and film industry. She nonchalantly shared that she worked for Tyler Perry Studios. In my mind I knew I was going to meet T. P. *Oookaay*, I thought in my Cardi B voice.

The house had five rooms; I chose the largest. I should have picked the room with the full-size bed, but I didn't. The twin-size bed made me feel like I was at least able to have some form of dorm life.

After we signed the necessary paperwork my sister and I brought all of my things to my new room and set it up. When finished, we went to Church's Chicken in the West End neighborhood and sat down to have lunch. I saw this one skinny Black, older, homeless man walking around with a woman's pink velour jogging suit on that was dirty in the booty part.

I looked at the man in disbelief and the scenery of the West End. It was just too much for me to take in at one time. I burst into tears at my new reality. I'd left all my friends, my church family, and everything familiar to chase after a decade-old dream. What the hell was I thinking? It came pouring out of my mouth. My face was flushed, I was hyperventilating, and my heart was heavy. I turned to my sister and said, "I hate Atlanta. It is hot, dirty, and I miss my friends. I hate it here." My sister looked at me thoughtfully and said, "Nell you are going to be OK. It is going to get better."

On our way back to the house we saw the same homeless man. He was clearly high on something. My sister looked over to see who I was studying so closely. We both looked at one another and said, simultaneously, "What the hell!" We both started laughing so hard we had tears in our eyes. I do not know who this man was, but he lightened up my mood. I know real men wear pink, but sir, why do your pants look like that only in the booty part?

You better not be walking around here pooping your pants. Homeless or not take your grown self to the bathroom. I was homeless before and you would never have known by looking at me. Everyone's situation is different, but man go to the bathroom, put you some cardboard or something down, but do not be in these streets like this.

My sister stayed the night with me in my room. I was dreading the next day because I knew she would be leaving to make the drive back to Florida. As my sister prepared to leave my mood was good. I was excited and optimistic about my future at Spelman.

I enjoyed mingling and bonding with my Spelman sisters on campus. During the first week of orientation all Spelman students were required to stay on campus one night. We stayed at the Living Learning Center, which housed the Bonner Scholars, Presidential Scholars, and other scholars.

Just before daybreak we experienced a special rite of passage that every Spelman woman experiences. It was unique, divine, and altogether inspiring.

This experience was so beautiful; I chose not to spoil it for my sisters. Just know when you get accepted into Spelman College, and you step on the campus, you will begin an extraordinary journey. Your life will never be the same. Get ready because you really are going to be prepared to change the world. Spelman will not make you become a leader or change agent, but it does help you become a better person by developing what is already in you.

Although Spelman works hard to be inclusive to all of their students, I later learned that being a commuter student definitely had its disadvantages. For me, it was not being able to enjoy campus life after hours as much as I wanted to. I found myself slightly irritated when I missed my opportunity to publicly introduce myself in the first week of orientation like so many of my sisters were able to. An announcement had gone out asking students to volunteer to be on a program for an opening ceremony. I must have missed the announcement commuting back and forth to campus.

I am going to be honest. At 400 pounds, my body was really struggling physically, walking back and forth in the heat to and from campus. Some days it took all I had in me to press my way back to campus. But there were also a couple of advantages to being a commuter student—the freedom to come and go freely and form connections with other students in the AUC. What I soon discovered about Al is that she only managed the house for her cousin and had better things to do than to hang out with us. She was nice, but on a few occasions, she came across a little stuck-up, so I only dealt with her when I needed to until she abruptly moved out.

For the life of me, I never understood how this Negro worked for Tyler Perry Studios and she ain't never go out her way to invite us to nothing. Good thing I went to Spelman, it was always crawling with inspiring Black people. I was running late for my Spanish class in the Cosby Building and literally almost bumped into actress Cassie Davis who was a part of my graduating class.

My mother made sure she told me she saw Tyler Perry and Steve Harvey at my graduation. I never saw them. Didn't I tell you I was totally focused on walking across the stage? I was trying to walk without falling; I was in so much pain and I was tired. My shoes did not quite fit. They were flopping around because I was walking on the back of the wedge-open toe heels. I thought to myself, *If I buy a simple pair of black shoelaces I can secure this shoe better and it will look more fashionable. They will look like they are supposed to string up my legs, but because I was already late I just could not risk being any later for my own graduation.*

Obviously, I was not able to have that dorm life experience with a group of my peers. That bond that many of my sisters were able to create through their dorm and twenty-four-hour campus life experience, I wish I'd had. I wish I'd been a part of Easter's Circle, a group of Christian women on campus. They formed an incredible sisterly bond.

My first year on campus the Holy Spirit did not give me permission to operate in my poetic spoken word gift. This made me feel like I missed out on bonding with other poets in the AUC. I had to trust that God had me in a season of hiding for a reason. I loved going to Jazzmine's Cafe on Thursday nights when it was open mic night, part of a movement of Black excellence going on through the performing and creative arts. It felt like a new version of what I can only imagine the Harlem Renaissance was like. The huge black and white pictures that hung on the walls invited you to take a walk down memory lane of Black history. The smoothies, sandwiches, pastries, and salads were also delicious and soothing as you embraced the poetic and harmonic sounds of the greatness of the AUC.

Being a transfer student meant that I simply had less time to enjoy many aspects of my college experience. In my second year, I had even less time than the average student. I was so busy focusing on trying to graduate with a documented learning disability, that I never fully took the time to smell the flowers by participating in as many activities and on-campus events as I would have liked.

Of course, navigating college life as a commuter student wasn't the only challenge I faced. The fear of rejection was also a problem.

I will never forget this quote by Benjamin E. Mays:

"It must be borne in mind that the tragedy of life doesn't lie in not reaching your goal. The tragedy lies in having no goal to reach. It isn't a calamity to die with dreams unfulfilled, but it is a calamity not to dream. It is not a disaster to be unable to capture your ideal, but it is a disaster to have no ideal to capture. It is not a disgrace not to reach the stars, but it is a disgrace to have no stars to reach for. Not failure, but low aim is a sin."

Every time I read this quote, it does something to me. It is as if it wills me to reach for the stars even if it looks impossible to everyone else, and even to myself at times. Never stop striving, dreaming, or daring to become greatness in motion. This quote helped me realize that I had to get over the fear of being rejected and the fear of failure if I was going to be successful in life.

As I went to register for my classes, a young lady informed me that every Spelman College student must take a class on the African Diaspora in the World (ADW). A slight wave of irritation arose within me when I learned that I had to take such a course.

What? What the hell are you talking about? I thought to myself. "I came in with an associate degree and I still have to take this course?"

I had researched the requirements for me to get accepted to Spelman and the classes needed in my major to graduate, how did I miss ADW?

I asked with as much attitude as could, "What is ADW?"

The woman looked at me as if to say, if you have to ask, then you should be taking the course. She choked down the slight laughter in her voice and replied, "ADW is the study of the African diaspora of the world.

In this class you will learn how the African diaspora has influenced every aspect of the world." I quickly turned away, irritated that I had missed that I needed to take this class, and embarrassed that I, as a Black woman, did not know what ADW stood for.

I loved my ADW class and can say hands down it was one of my favorite classes at Spelman, after Black Theology and Intro to Islam. I will never forget that in class we had to do a group project on how people rebelled against slavery in their own ways. My group chose to put slavery on trial. In doing so we interviewed different historical women who chose to rebel or become change agents in the fight for equality. It was liberating and informative. One slave was on trial for killing her slave master. We learned that many Black women rebelled against slavery in their own ways.

I wrote a paper on the patriarchal system of the world, based on Elizabeth Jenkins' book *Harriet*, comparing it to James Brown's song, "This is a Man's World." I described how we live in a patriarchal world that tends to forget the rest of the lyrics to this song, "but it would be nothing without a woman, or a girl." I did so well in that class that my professor handpicked me and some of my peers to apply to a study abroad program in Trinidad and Tobago.

I never thought in my wildest dreams that attending Spelman would present me with my first opportunity to travel out of the country.

I was excited about the possibility of studying abroad, but I was also nervous because no one in my immediate family had been out of the country or had the resources for me to travel internationally. One of my family members even remarked, "You should be happy with going to Spelman. You always wanna do everything!"

Basically, that family member wanted me to settle for what I'd already accomplished.

My sister Nada fanned the flame of my dream. She helped me by dropping off sponsorship packages and telling others to purchase my poetry. Almost every other day my sister would wake up and tell me about the dreams she had about someone donating a certain amount of money to me to study abroad. Every time she had a dream it happened just as she had dreamt it, except for the fact that most of my sister's dreams involved people of a different gender than the person who actually fulfills the dream. For example, if she dreamed that a woman gave $500, a man would donate it, or vice versa.

I woke up early every morning and went to bed late working on my goal and dream of studying abroad. My sister looked at me and said, *"I* damn sho' hope you get to go. Cause when I say you deserve it! You done work yo' ass off. You deserve it." My sister witnessed all of the hard work and sacrifices I made. She saw me crying through my frustration, the rejections, and donations that did not quite add up.

At the end of the day, God provided for me and I was able to study abroad. It was an experience that I will never forget. I was excited and ready to experience something new and bond with my Spelman sisters.

Eight of us participated in the program at the University of the West Indies.

While there I was shocked to learn that one of my Spelman Sisters was pregnant, yet the school had still allowed her to study abroad. I found myself amazed by her drive not to be another statistic. She worked hard during her free time to ensure that she secured an apartment, childcare, and her classes for the next semester. I remember that her plan was to have her baby and be back in class three days later.

A few years ago, I smiled when I saw her wedding picture on social media. I never doubted her. She was one of the most driven and focused students in our group.

The water in Trinidad and Tobago was so beautiful and inviting. My grandmother, along with many others, believed that the Caribbean waters had healing power. For the most part, the weather was nice. It was beautiful, sunny, and tropical. I loved our community kitchen, a patio kitchen on the third floor of the campus apartments, where we prepared meals to enjoy outside on the balcony.

I was ignorant of many aspects of Caribbean culture back then. Before I arrived, I thought I was going to see a lot of Black people. I remember walking around in the airport and being shocked at the number of Indian people I saw. Later that week, in my class "Caribbean History and Civilization," I learned about indentured servants and how other ethnic groups became a part of the Caribbean.

I fell in love with the Trinidadian culture. I found myself amazed as I went on excursions to places like the Floating Temple, old rum factories where slaves worked, and other historical and natural landmarks. The waterfalls were breathtaking. I absolutely hated the way the people drove there yet found it fascinating that they were able to drive on the left side of the road.

When grocery shopping, it took me a minute to get used to finding milk on the shelf rather than in refrigerated coolers. I hated the ground beef there because it always crumbled and fell apart. I tried everything to make it hold together, but nothing worked. I thought I was going to lose it when I found out that there was no McDonald's on the entire Island. The locals said the concept of a Big Mac did not do well there. From the looks of it neither was I if I did not get a burger soon.

KPL warned us not to be "Ugly Americans!" a name Americans earned if they were rude or acted entitled while abroad. I am not going to lie; as much as I love traveling to other countries and experiencing other cultures, there is no place like America. In Trinidad there was no concept of customer service, something that I as an American was used to. If you asked to speak to a manager, their attitude was worse than the employee's.

I secretly wondered how I would enjoy the island in my free time. Would I meet new people? Would I find a little church to visit? Man, was the food going to be good? Would I meet the man of my dreams and get swept off my feet? *OK, maybe not the last part, but a girl can dream.* I had already told myself I was not going to be talking to any foreigners because *they were not about to be dating me to get a green card.* Whewww child! Nobody was checking for me. The one guy I danced with at the club got no talk time from me. I was embarrassed by the way he was grinding on me.

I whispered to my friend Brooklyn, "He is grinding on me, and he is on hard." I was done dancing in the packed smoke-filled club.

Brooklyn replied, "Girrrl, it's a problem if he's not."

I had enough of my Spelman Sisters convincing me, the most conservative one out the group into trying a bunch of mess. Leave it up to Jeter, the smallest one out of the bunch, little Ms. Daredevil, we all will be jumping out of planes. Not to mention I almost drowned listening to Bri at the beach earlier today.

"Tanell-Tanell, when the wave comes, jump up."

Baby, that wave came and just call me Mikie I jumped up, but the wave was so big, I lost my footing. Then more waves slammed into me, dragging me down the beach.

I could hear myself talking to God in my mind, as panic set in. *God help I cannot die in Trinidad.* I was trying with all my might to get up. Every time I tried; another wave hit me. My knees were scraped and slightly bleeding. I was choking on water and gasping for air.

Damn! I could not believe it. I heard in my spirit, *"If you do not stand up, you are going to die."* I know to this day it was only God who saved me. When I finally stood up and was able to get my bearings, I noticed a piece of my hair weave floating next to me. I was so mad at my Spelman Sisters, I just wanted to go down the line and smack them all upside their heads. Those fools thought it was funny. I was the only person not laughing.

While in the Caribbean I told myself, *You have to speak here. You know you were called to be an international speaker and preacher.* I whispered to myself to be intentional. If you speak here, you can say you are an international speaker and you have international speaking experience. I performed some of my poetry there and received a standing ovation.

I have always felt most alive when I am speaking. It is as if the entire world is sitting still waiting for me to say something profound.

I remember when Holy Spirit first told me I was going to be a motivational speaker. I was afraid to tell anyone because I was embarrassed and thought motivational speakers did not make any money. I remember finally telling my uncle what Holy Spirit told me and why I chose to hide it. He said, "Girl, are you crazy? Do you know how much motivational speakers make? Have you never heard of Les Brown? Girrrrl! I looked like I was stuck on stupid because he was right.

I knew nothing about motivational speakers except that they give speeches to inspire people. That night I learned a valuable lesson in the importance of doing research and honing your craft. You owe it to yourself to be knowledgeable about your skills, gifts, and talents.

Pearls of Wisdoms

Living My Dream

- Never allow your dreams to expire or slip through your fingers.
- Fight for your dreams with all of your might.
- In order for you to live out your dreams you must be willing to make the sacrifices needed to maintain them.
- Be OK with being the only person in the room with your divine, unique, physical, mental, spiritual, and emotional makeup.
- Strive to be socially, emotionally, mentally, physically, and spiritually fit to live out your dreams.
- Live out your dreams without regrets.
- As you are living out your dreams, remember to laugh and have fun.

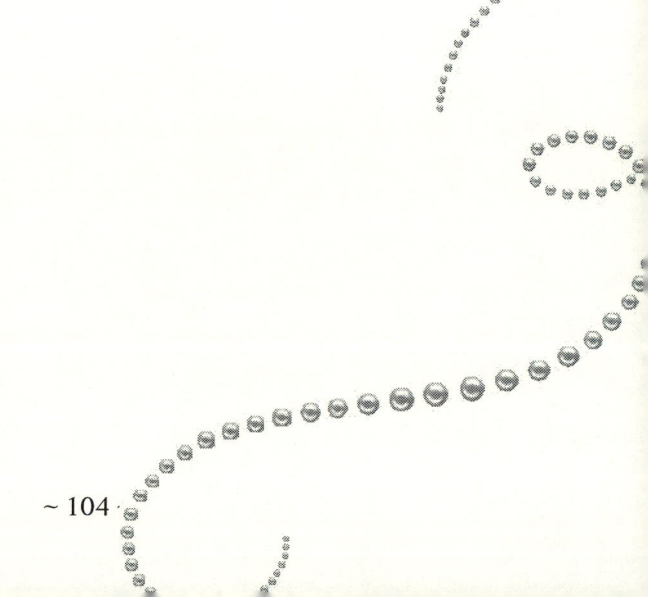

Chapter 15

History in the Making

> *My President is Black, my Lambo's blue...*
> —Young Jeez

During my senior year at Spelman, I witnessed and played an active role in making history. Who would have thought that we would see Dr. Martia Luther King Jr.'s famous "I Have a Dream" speech come to fruition with the election of our first Black President, Barack Obama, in 2009. Campus life buzzed with currents of change, sending shock waves through our student body. Most of us beamed with pride, excitement, and a tinge of fear.

We beamed with pride to have a Black man running for office during our generation. Some of us were bubbling with excitement because there were a couple of excellent candidates running for office regardless of the color of their skin or their gender.

I was excited that Hilary Rodham Clinton decided to run for the American presidency. I always thought that she was a remarkable woman. But I was especially impressed with Obama. Everything about him seemed well-polished, educated, articulate, classy, and honorable.

As an African American woman, I knew why he had to work hard and behave in a manner that was above reproach. Growing up in the South I learned about "Black Tags as Child." These are the things that identify us as being other. Black people still have to be intentional in removing the "Black Tags" off of us and we still have to work two to three times harder than our white counterparts to be deemed as qualified.

I carefully pondered who to vote for. I did not want to vote for a candidate based solely on their political party, their gender, or the color of their skin. There were some who urged and tried to pressure others to vote for Obama because he was a Black man.

I knew he was well-qualified for the job, but there was still something in me that felt like I needed to put this honestly before God, since I did not want to vote for him just because he was a Black man. I prayed and asked God to help me. *God, I honestly do not know who to vote for. I want to vote for the best candidate for the position.*

I was lying in my bed sleeping and God showed me President Barack Obama. I saw him just before the sun came up and before he started his day, he was kneeling on one knee, and praying to God for wisdom. At that moment I knew he was the best candidate to sit in the highest office of the American government. He reminded me of King Solomon, who was wise and humble enough to know that he could not lead God's people without God's wisdom.

I learned a valuable lesson that day. If ever we are bold enough to ask God a question, we must be humble enough to receive and trust His answer.

Some of the older people I knew were fearful about Obama becoming president due to the possibility of him being assassinated.

Some of those silver-haired people had lived through the assassination of some of our greatest civil rights leaders. They knew firsthand how far we had come, yet how much further still we needed to go.

Dr. Johnetta Betsch Cole, former President of Spelman College, posits that "racism is the stench of America's dirty laundry." If not separated and cleaned properly, stenches have a way of making clean clothes smell dirty and or look murky.

I understood why some older people were fearful, but I also knew that the calling of greatness had to be bigger than the feelings of fear that tugged at the corners of peoples' hearts. This is when we do what Joyce Myers so eloquently says, "Do it afraid!"

If Obama had allowed the fear of failure to overtake him, he would not have made history or lived out the manifestation of Dr. King's dream. Yet, he did more than that. He showed many children of color that they too could one day become president. He gave them permission to dare to dream big and pursue their purpose, even if it had never been done before. That they could be the one who makes, or changes history, with their story.

Pearls of Wisdom

History in the Making

- I may be the first to make history, but I won't be the last.
- The sacrifices I make today will help me and others tomorrow.
- I am a legend in the making.
- Never allow fear to stop you from trying to do what you have been called to do and from your purpose in life.
- Acknowledging one's fears and working through them gives others permission to do the same.
- God has positioned you to be a change agent, and your assignment is to bring forth the change needed to equip generations with the tools to execute the greatness within them.
- It is always important to consult God before making critical decisions.
- True success requires us to put some skin in the game. It is never easy, but necessary.
- The sooner you embrace your individual learning style, your creativity, your beauty, and your personality, the more self-aware you will become.

Chapter 16

When Man Says No but God Says Yes!

> *All access granted!*
> —Anonymous

Matriculating through college with a learning disability was not easy. Many people felt that I would not be successful in college. I was the main individual who constantly doubted my abilities. I had to learn how to not be my own worst enemy, and as my English professor Susan Ford would say, "Girly, get out of your own way." As I've explained I had to find my own learning style, ask the right questions, and flip the label to make it work for me. In knowing my own learning style, it was as if God was showing me, that everything I thought I could not do, I could do.

While in college I discovered that whenever it comes to learning I have a peak performance time, a time where I am the most focused and most alert. For me this is 3:00 a.m. to 6:00 a.m. This is a spiritual and natural discipline I live by to this day. I also learned that giving myself fake deadlines was essential to completing projects on time without cramming. This required me to thoroughly understand my assignments.

I also learned that not everyone can teach me. God revealed to me, *Tanell this is why we have different pastors, and why everyone does not have the same pastor, pastors, or denomination.* People require different styles of leadership, education, and relationships. Someone being unable to teach me does not mean they are a bad educator, it simply means that their teaching style may not be most effective for my style of learning.

These simple tweaks improved my learning style and reminded me that when "Man says no, God says yes!" It also illustrated how with God's wisdom and instructions, and with me disciplining myself, there is nothing I cannot do.

Annabel was the learning disability specialist at ECC who took the time to help me understand and normalize my learning style. I hated math with a passion because it often left me feeling confused and frustrated. I just didn't get it. Annabel was the first person who taught me to use colored paper to help me focus. This was essential for me because sometimes having a learning disability made it hard for me to focus in school.

Oftentimes, I struggled with showing how I got the right answer. I would work on the problems backwards; I would start with the answer but could not show how I arrived at it. Too many steps confused me, especially when I did not know how I got to the answer. It took me a while before I realized I had a form of math dyslexia. I am a *why* learner; I have to know and understand why I am doing something in order for it to make sense to me. When I can grasp the why factor in learning, I do well in that subject.

I learned to meet with professors prior to taking their classes to introduce myself and thoroughly review the course syllabus with them.

This helps both of us become familiar with each other and our respective teaching and learning styles. It also allows me to see whether the professors are going to play an active role in fostering my individual learning style and ultimately helps me determine whether I should take the class or a different one. In some ways it's an interview, for both of us.

There were some classes I still took just to challenge myself. Spanish was a language I always wanted to learn.

I took Spanish for six years straight and struggled the entire time. When I got to Spelman, there was an extraordinary learning disability services program that valued and took into consideration each student's individual style.

While at Spelman, Ms. McDonald was my disability specialist. She always reminded me of a cross between a therapist and an elder. Her skin was the color of warm golden honey that had been kissed by the sun in some places. She had a head full of salt-and-pepper hair that mesmerized me. Not a hair was ever out of place. I was not quite sure if her hair was permed or pressed, but it was beautiful just like her spirit. She was warm, friendly, and always professional. Her eyes always seemed to drink you in as she engaged in active and intuitive listening.

One day as we were discussing my classes she informed me, "Tanell, due to your learning disability, you may not have to take Spanish." I repeated, "I may not have to take Spanish!?" For a moment, I was relieved, I could have done a victory lap even at 400 lbs. Then I took a moment to gather my thoughts.

"No!" I proclaimed, in one of the most stubborn and determined voices within me. I knew that avoiding Spanish would be me taking the easy way out. "No, I want to take Spanish!" So, I took it and struggled through it.

I wrote labels on things in Spanish. I would go days on with my TV on Spanish speaking channels, got my Morehouse brothers to tutor me, and I devoted extra time studying to comprehend the language.

Pearls of Wisdom

When Man Says No but God Says Yes!

- Remember that God is the author of your life's story and you are the co-author.
- No goal is unobtainable if it is part of your purpose.
- You were created to manifest the glory of God's greatness.
- God has the final say.
- A plot twist is not the end of your story, it is just a change that you did not see coming.

Chapter 17

Faith Laced with Grief and Depression

> *I found that with depression, one of the most important things you can realize is you're not alone...You're not the first person to go through it; you're not going to be the last to go through it...Hold onto that fundamental quality of faith. Have faith that on the other side of your pain [or grief] is something good.*
>
> —*Dwayne 'The Rock' Johnson*

T**his damn cape is choking.** I do not think I fully took the time I needed to deal with the loss of my brother Jeremy. Some people told me that it was time to get over it, to change my voicemail where I recited poetry in his honor: *"The media, naysayers, and critics tried to destroy your image, I will make sure your legacy makes it past the line of scrimmage. You might be gone, but you will never be forgotten, rest in heavenly eternal peace, Jeremy Hason Henry.*

After losing Jeremy, I allowed two things to consume me, which were my faith in God, and my dream to attend Spelman. In many ways, I focused on those things as coping mechanisms and distractions from dealing with losing him. At the forefront and back of my mind I focused on him being proud of me for achieving my dream.

Once I achieved the dream of getting into Spelman, what would be next? After a month or so of being at Spelman College, I sunk into depression like never before. I slept a lot; I was irritable and moody. I thought it was the pressure of being a "Spelman Woman," but it was so much more than that.

Yes, some of it was because I had not dealt with and adequately grieved my brother's death. Another huge factor was I suffered from undiagnosed depression all of my life. I never knew what I was feeling was called. The grief and depression were affecting my mental well-being. My momma described depression as a gray area. I remember her telling me, "You are either strong or weak, black or white. Tanell, there is no gray area."

My mother did not know anything about counseling or therapy when I was a kid. I think I was in the fourth or fifth grade when I noticed these different kinds of funks I would go through. This was during the era of *What goes on in this house stays in this house.*

There were always three things that pulled me out of my funks. My faith, through hearing the word of God, watching Black award shows on TV, and reading positive and affirming Black publications.

These things made me believe that I could be and do anything. I found inspiration flipping through my Auntie Nae-nae's collections of *Ebony*, *Essence*, and *Jet* magazines. I aspired to be like so many of the Black women who graced their covers and told their stories.

At an early age I recognized the power that media, creative, and performing arts had on me. They helped me to cope with depression, yet I did not really know how to say I felt better after hearing "Still I Rise" or seeing the *Essence Awards*. It was something I could not explain.

You would think after I'd been able to live out my dream of attending Spelman that things would be perfect. But instead, during my first semester depression hit me like a wrecking ball. I could not explain how I felt to anyone. I was afraid to talk to anyone about it because a lot of people were so proud of me and I did not want to let them down. There were others who were waiting for me to flunk out. I had lost my motivation and passion for everything. I was chronically late for class, missing assignments, and I could feel my dream slipping through my fingers.

Sometimes, the fear of failure was so crippling that I was unable to even try to move forward. I had to ask myself some tough questions, and I had to be willing to put in the work to access my healing.

- Why am I so afraid of failing?
- Why am I still embarrassed about having a learning disability?
- Why am I self-sabotaging my own success?
- What is this heaviness I am feeling?
- What does it look like for me to get help?
- Who can I ask for help?
- How can I use the help without becoming dependent?
- How can I use the arts as a therapeutic outlet for help with the heaviness, and how can I draw inspiration from the arts?
- How can I use my faith to build my confidence in the areas I feel less competent in?

These were the thought-provoking questions that I asked myself.

They may seem simple to some people, but for me asking and reflecting on them meant that I was putting in the work to be successful from a holistic approach. I have always found inspiration and motivation through self-reflection.

If you were to take a moment to ask yourself only three thought-provoking questions to help you become unstuck, find motivation, and find inspiration what would the questions be? Very good Charlie Brown! Now that you are becoming aware of these tools, how are you going to use them to help cultivate growth and development?

Pearls of Wisdom

Faith Laced with Grief and Depression

- Find out why you are afraid of failing and explore ways you can overcome that fear.

- Get over being embarrassed by the labels others place on you. You can take them off by speaking positive affirmations over your life.

- Get out of your own way. Do this by taking advantage of every opportunity that comes your way. Don't allow yourself to talk yourself out of trying to do new things.

- Step out of your comfort zone.

- Be unapologetically willing to explore why you feel a certain way.

- Be OK with your journey of healing and wholeness and being different from others.

- Recognize your tribe, your divine team, and your sacred circle of influencers.

- Lean and depend solely on God.

- God is your source; everything and everyone else are resources.

- Therapeutic outlets vary from person to person, so use what speaks to your soul and feeds your purpose.

- You can use your faith to build your confidence by reading, writing, and speaking your confidence into existence.

- You must feed and nourish anything that you want to grow.

Chapter 18

"Harpo, Who That Man Is"

> *When someone shows you who they are, believe them.*
> —Dr. Maya Angelou

I often say this, but I think at times it falls on deaf ears. Talking, dating, sleeping with, and marrying the wrong person can change the trajectory of your whole life. Look at some of these celebrity couples. They should have never been together, but because of the industry they are in, someone may have been hyping them up or encouraging them to engage in a relationship that became toxic and abusive—for the sake of publicity.

Sometimes it can be the pressure of an environment, people such as family and friends, people who look good on Christian paper. Or it can be you who settles for low-hanging fruit. And if we are really being honest, the fear of being alone makes us put up with people and things we don't even like.

I was totally shocked when I did not catch the eye of one of my Morehouse Brothers. I had a crush on this guy named Hilman at Morehouse. He was intelligent, nice, tall-dark-and-fresh-out-the-barbershop-looking.

He was on the football team. I found myself smitten by him. When we first met, I noticed he kept staring at me. I was not really sure why.

I asked, "What are you staring at?"

He shook his head and replied, "Nothing!"

We talked briefly in the Cosby Building. We both found something intriguing about the other, yet we could not quite put our finger on it. It was like there was some form of magnetic pull between us. We ended up bumping into each other a few more times that day on Spelman's campus. The last time our eyes looked in on each other that day was upstairs in the Manely Building around the corner from the cafeteria.

"What?" I asked, curiously.

He shrugged his massive shoulders to answer my question. From that moment on I was crushing on Hilman.

My friend Ms. Pris-pris had helped me create this online account where I was able to send him messages. And for weeks I sent him private messages about how much I liked him and that I had a crush on him. I gave him clues about who I was without revealing my identity. He tried hard to figure out who I was and how we met. I told my closest friends about him and they were all cheering me on.

I was excited about the possibility of having a budding romance with him, until I found out he was crushing on some pregnant girl in my Old Testament class. I overheard her mention his name as she chatted with another student: "Hilman keeps trying to talk to me, Girrrl!"

I was clearly not eavesdropping, but when I heard his name my body stiffened and my ears perked up. I looked her up and down with sheer shock. I could hardly believe that a guy of his caliber would be interested in a girl who was already around four or five months pregnant with someone else's child. I could not help but insert myself into the conversation.

I asked, "Are you talking about Hilman on the football team that lives in Perdue Hall?"

She replied, with a matter-of-fact attitude, "Yesss, I am!"

She looked as if she wanted to say, "And what is it to you?"

I recognized the tension that was hanging in the air and smiled it off. "He likes you, and he knows you're pregnant?"

"Yep! These niggas don't care!"

My mouth almost flew open, but my eyes widened with pure emotion. I felt like someone was just jumping up and down on my heart. I was hurt that my crush actually had a crush on someone else. I was broken-hearted over a guy who never once said he liked me or was even attracted to me.

It made me really question my appearance. I did not fully understand why I was seen as only a platonic Spelman Sister. My Morehouse Brothers only saw me as a sister to hang out with, to tell their secrets to, to pray for them, to encourage them, or even worse to serve as a beard or some of them that were gay, and nothing more. I had made peace with the idea that my Morehouse Brothers never saw me as anything more than a sister or a friend. Even though a few of them joked about marrying me after hearing my poetry, a joke was all it was.

One day while walking from Jazzmine's café. I met this guy who worked at Morehouse and we started talking. When we started dating,

I thought I had found a bird's nest on the ground. We hit it off quickly, but he really was a predator disguised as Prince Charming.

Winston (or Win, as we called him) had a winning smile and most people who met him liked him. He was tall, had a muscular build, brown skin, and was clean-cut with dreamy-looking eyes that fooled most people. My friend and Spelman sister Milli loved him. I mean, he did make sure he brought her some vegan food every time he knew she was coming around.

He was always very thoughtful and polite. His coworkers liked him and spoke highly of him. One of his old high school female classmates, who worked at Spelman, spoke well of him. In fact, nobody ever said one bad thing about him except for one lady who worked in the cafeteria at Spelman. I saw her watching my man and me talking and having a good time. I wondered to myself why she was watching us like that.

She saw me later that week and asked me, "Do you know him?"

I answered, "Yes, he's my boyfriend."

She cautioned, "You need to leave him alone. He has a lot of kids, and he is crazy."

I had a dream about him raping one of my housemates. I prayed and asked God to show me the Spirit behind his face. God did just that. I don't think I really wanted to see all of what God showed me about him. Winston was a wolf in sheep's clothing who had been stealing things from my room while we were dating. Not major things like my bank cards, social security number, or cash. It was small things he knew I would never bother to look for or miss.

I remember feeling excited and uncomfortable the very first time I went to his home in College Park. Something led me to tell my sister and Pastor Faith where I was going.

I used to be so naive about people and so trusting, until my young brother Jeremy was murdered. After that, I knew that people could and would do anything to anybody given the space and opportunity.

I always prayed and talked to God about how young women were brutally raped and murdered. I always asked for His divine hedge of protection and discernment of people. This insight has saved my life and kept me alive.

As Win and I prepared to go to his apartment I fumbled around my bedroom thinking to myself, *I have not stayed the night at a guy's house since I dated My Muse, my ex who lived in Chicago. What if I am making a mistake?* I could hear my friend Evy's voice in my head again, *"Nellie there you go again lacing up those track shoes to run again."* Shhhhash!!! I am not running! Dammmit Man! I am just thinking. For the love of God and all that is Holy! Can a Sista just think?

Her running joke for me was that I was a runner. She dubbed me "The Track Star Dater." It secretly bothered me that she thought of me as a Track Star Dater because I wanted to be in a relationship and fall in love with *the one*, but the slightest thing a man did made me lace up my running shoes.

I silenced all the wild thoughts running rampant in my mind as I studied my face in the mirror for a moment. I looked away as I grabbed the razor off the vanity table and said to myself, low enough for him to hear, *"I should take my razor with me."* Win's eyes were animated with shock. "Wooooooo!" he said. "What do you need a razor for?" I shrugged, "I'll just leave it here."

I put the razor back on the vanity table that doubled as a desk. Once we'd walked out of the house, I made an excuse to go back to my room. I quickly wrapped the blade in a small piece of paper towel and stuck it in my bra. I dashed outside to meet Win. As soon as we started waiting on the train, I became very gassy.

I was like Big Momma in the movie *Big Momma's House*. "When I got to go, I got to go!" We could not stop, because we were waiting on the last running train to his house in College Park.

He held my hands as I cried and prayed that at 30, I would not poop on myself in public in front of my boyfriend. Those prayers worked because I did not!

As I began to settle in at Win's apartment, I began to notice some of my belongings here and there, like they belonged to him. Without meaning to I shouted, "Wait one damn minute!" It startled both of us. Win's head quickly whipped around. I did not recognize my own voice as I spoke. I was pissed off that this dude had stolen these items from my house.

I asked him, "Did you take these towels, and my house shoes from my room?" "Yes," he replied calmly. "I didn't think you would mind."

"I do mind because you did not ask me," I responded back.

Although Win apologized and I forgave him, there was something about him that made me wonder about him from that point on. This was the first time we'd slept in the same bed with space and opportunity between the two of us.

Win started developing what I thought of as disappearing acts. I soon learned that he suffered from seizures. He claimed this was why he was sometimes missing in action. One day after having lunch with me on campus, he said, "A detective left her card on my door. I wonder what she wanted. "Baby, let me use your phone to call her." She started calling my phone looking for him. It was as if they were playing phone tag. They would literally miss each other by minutes. I remember asking the detective, "Can I ask what this phone call is in regard to?"

She said, "No ma'am. I cannot tell you that. Please have him call me back. "OK", I answered dryly. As I hung up the phone, I decided to call Evy and get her opinion on the matter. I shared with her about Win and the detective playing phone tag. I said, "Girl, how are people married to serial killers and never know or suspect a thing?" She replied, "Esheee! I know!" We both laughed at the irony and reality of it. I went on, "Girl that could not be me. I'm going to investigate. Do you think I should call the detective back to see what she can share with me?"

"Nellie, it couldn't hurt."

I sighed. "OK. Pray for me."

I called the detective back and formally introduced myself to her. "Hello, my name is Tanell Vashawn Allen. Winston is my boyfriend. My parents sent me away to attend Spelman College. If I were your daughter, would you want me to date Winston?"

She replied, "No, I would not." I didn't know what was going on, but she was too confident in her answer.

I replied, "Thank you, good night."

The next day, Win walked me to Praise Team practice in the rain with a giant umbrella. I let him borrow my phone to sort out whatever was going on with him and the detective. I kept in mind what she'd said the previous night. Win was very charming and thoughtful. He knew how to win people over through acts of service and quality time, which are two of my love languages.

He came back to pick me up after practice a little later than I'd expected, but he assured me that the matter had been cleared up. He told me that he was going to be on his way to meet with the detective to give a statement. He got me dinner, gave me money, and gave me his link card and PIN number to order groceries. At that moment nothing seemed odd because he'd always done things for me. He asked me to call the detective to tell her he was on his way and what he was wearing.

I called her and did as I was instructed. When I got to the part about him being on his way to meet her and to give her his statement, she corrected me. "No ma'am, he is not giving a statement, he is being charged with two accounts of rape and kidnapping."

The room must have started spinning because I felt dizzy, lightheaded, and sick to my stomach. "What? What did you just say?" I asked, but hearing it a second time was not going to lighten up the blow.

She stated, "Ms. Allen, I need you to come down to the station and give a statement."

I replied, "OK!" But I couldn't do it. The shame and embarrassment I felt was gut-wrenching. What if he had raped one of my female housemates or one of Spelman Sisters? I don't know if I would have been able to live with that. Looking back on the situation, I see that there were so many red flags about Win that I had ignored.

He used to tell me, "I am going to take you to my house, tie you up, rape you, and have my way with you." I never took him seriously when he said this from time to time. I would always tell him, "The devil is a lie. You are not going to do anything to me." I always meant what I said when I spoke to him or any other man due to my mother being a domestic violence victim.

I never worried about being raped by Win. He was always a gentleman with me except for the one time we were being intimate and I told him to stop, but he kept going. I pushed him off me and smacked the hell out of him.

I felt like part of him wanted to see how I would react. Well, he found out! It never crossed my mind that he could be a rapist. Maybe because I told myself, "You cannot rape the willing." Yet, I find that statement perplexing because you can rape the willing if they are forced, coerced, manipulated, or chemically influenced to sleep with you.

I have always heard, "Rape is about control." In our relationship, Win portrayed himself as the perfect gentleman, yet he was a sexual predator. He was very cunning and charming, but I never allowed him to have any control over me. After he was charged with rape the shame and guilt of his actions did control me in some ways.

The emotional trauma of finding out that my boyfriend was a rapist and that I'd contracted my first STD from him was difficult for me to stomach. I was ashamed to walk on the Morehouse campus because many of his coworkers knew we were dating each other. I had to make a conscious decision not to allow Win's ill-mannered actions to rob my present and future social and academic interactions.

I walked into Kilgore's Cafe with my head held high, knowing that some of the cafeteria workers would recognize me.

Whoop, there it goes! I silently said to myself as I watched an older black lady with a hairnet whisper to her coworker. She cupped her hand over her mouth, trying to be discreet. As if she knew I was an expert at lip reading. Her body language gave her away. I was ready to address anybody and everybody who had something to say.

I was not going to avoid this situation anymore. I purposely went through her line. She finally built up enough courage to ask me, "Ain't you the gal that goes with Win?" I looked her sternly in the eyes and said, "Yes, I was. Until he got around here and started raping women. Win is in jail where he belongs."

She looked at me as if she was surprised by my boldness and honesty. Yet there was something about my statement that earned her respect and approval.

I felt like Anika Noni Rose's character Lorrell Robinson from the movie *Dream Girls*. "I ain't no girl anymore. I am a woman!" A woman who had suffered one of the worst forms of embarrassment from a man, in my mind, yet I chose not to allow it to overtake me.

I promised myself that one day I would deal with this emotional trauma and I would allow myself to enter another relationship and entertain the idea of falling in love with who God has for me. But for now, I was just trying to make it across the stage to graduate. For me to do so, I had to resort back to the same coping mechanisms I had used so many times in the past. I had to push my emotional trauma down deep within me and power through what I was dealing with. If I tried to stop and process this emotional trauma without God and a trained professional, I would have had a nervous breakdown.

I told myself that women before me, my momma, my sister, and my grandmamma, have been through worse and they still made it to the other side. If they did it, so can I. God built me to last. I cannot afford to drop the ball at 30 years old. It took me too long to accomplish this dream to allow it to slip through my fingers; I was too close to the finish line.

I can see it. I know I can do it. I just need a few more weeks of having tunnel vision. I am unstoppable. God, give me strength to present my thesis on how Black women use their faith as a coping mechanism to deal with stress and depression. If ever there was a time to live out my thesis next to the death of my brother, this would be it. I can do all things through Christ.

Pearls of Wisdom

"Harpo Who That Man Is?"

- ➢ Always listen to Holy Spirit, or your gut feeling, when assessing who people are despite who they appear to be.

- ➢ Do not allow other people's shame to become yours.

- ➢ Take as much time as you need to embrace your journey of healing and wholeness.

- ➢ No one has the right to disrespect you or exploit your body.

- ➢ Be OK with setting personal boundaries that are inviolable.

- ➢ Never throw pearls of wisdom away.

- ➢ Never show a person your heart or share your bed with a person you don't fully trust, or with a person whose intentions you're not sure of.

- ➢ Always try your best to keep your promises, especially to God and to yourself.

- ➢ Soul-care is just as important as self-care.

Chapter 19

Laying on of Hands

> "Sister let me see your hands..."
> -*Anonymous*

Leading up to graduation I had to present my thesis to the Religious Studies Department. My thesis explored how African American women used their faith as a coping mechanism to deal with stress and depression. I was passionate about this topic because I was living proof of it. I felt nervous and scared about defending my thesis because I still struggled with formal academic writing.

Not only did I have to present my thesis to the Religious Studies committee, but I also had to present it to a group of my peers. I knew that my thesis was an excellent subject to discuss and would be beneficial to others. I was hanging onto the hope of having the opportunity to be able to orally defend my thesis. I prayed it would work out in my favor considering that I had talent as an orator and had excelled at persuasive speaking.

You would have never known this about me in the past. I spent over half of my childhood in speech therapy. When I was in the eighth grade, I heard one of my friends recite the speech "To Soar." When I heard it, I fell in love with public speaking. I did not stop studying it until I learned every word of that three-page speech to perfection.

As I began defending my thesis my right hand began to tremble slightly. That was my tell-tell that I was nervous. As I sat at the head of the table, I started speaking. For the first time, I spoke openly about the effects of choking down my grief and trauma of having lost my brother. how not fully dealing with it, coupled with living in fear of failure, caused me to put living my dream in jeopardy. The very thing I was most fearful of was about to happen. If it was not for my faith, divine intervention, and me writing therapeutically, I would have flunked out of Spelman.

As I defended my thesis confidently and boldly, a sense of pride came over me because I knew that all the sacrifices, I had made were worth it. I had many sleepless nights and early morning homework sessions, often leading to mental and emotional breakdowns. When it comes to learning, I have always been my own worst enemy. I was constantly at war within myself about my ability to meet academic requirements. As a child I was conditioned to believe that intellectually, I was not able to learn like others and that being learning-disabled meant that I was incapable of learning.

After presenting and answering my committee members' and peers' questions, the room erupted in a round of applause. I kind of set the bar high for the person who had to present after me. She looked impressed, but she was not confident in her ability to rise to the occasion. She seemed slightly happy that I went over my time, leaving her with less time to present.

I felt so relieved after defending my thesis! I knew that the worst was behind me. But I still was stressed out because I was still trying to get into the Intensive Spanish Program at Morehouse. I was praying that I would be accepted into this program so that I could meet my graduation requirements.

What irritated me about the director of this program was her biased behavior. I applied for the program early and met all the requirements, but she still did not pick me for the program. I knew during the interview she was not going to pick me. I wanted to be petty and keep the program to myself, but Holy Spirit would not let me. It hurt me to see people I recommended to the program get accepted. Some of them did not even need to take the class to graduate that year, and there were others who really did not care whether they got accepted or not.

Yet I cared and I needed to be accepted to this program to officially graduate on time and to get accepted to graduate school. Otherwise I was going to have to pay out of pocket to take Spanish 201 and 202 at Atlanta Metro Community College. I could feel my dream of graduating on time and attending grad school slipping through my fingers. All I could do was pray to God to get into the program, or I was going to be in summer school.

The ending of one chapter in our life can be difficult to handle. I knew I was graduating from Spelman College, and that I would go from being a woman of Spelman to being a Spelman Woman. What life would look like after graduation was still a little fuzzy for me. I needed God to show me clearly what my next move would be.

I had applied to Duke Divinity School. I visited its beautiful campus, but there was something about attending graduate school there that didn't feel right to my spirit.

I was assured Duke wanted me and would give me financial support, but I intentionally had not submitted my transcripts to them and was placed on their waiting list.

I got accepted into Emory Theological Seminary and was awarded a scholarship. But during my campus visit, as soon as I stepped out of the car and my feet hit the concrete, I could feel the campus' energy and knew Emory was not the right fit for me. If I had attended grad school there I would not have graduated, or it would have taken longer because mentally and socially it was not the right fit for me. I decided that neither Duke or Emory was for me.

Graduation was rapidly approaching, but I was not ready for the next step. My dream since the 11th grade had been to attend Spelman College. I'd never dreamed past that point though. I felt like Oprah Winfrey when she shared her story about being a poor little Black girl and counting the trees in some rich White people's yard. She always dreamed of having 10 trees, but she was blessed with over 3,000 trees. She asserts, "God's dream for me was bigger than the dream I could have imagined for myself."

During the week of my graduation, I remember feeling more and more overwhelmed and stressed out by my uncertainty. But there was a church service, *The Laying of Hands by the Elders,* that gave me peace. At this service our professor and ministers prayed for us, spoke blessings over us, gave us pearls of wisdom, covered us spiritually, and released us into the next chapter of our purpose.

It was all so beautiful. As we sat, the professors and ministers came to us and laid their hands on our shoulders and prayed. They took time to minister to our needs individually and collectively. The greatest sense of peace came over me.

I cried in the arms of a beautiful, slightly older dark-skinned woman. She was tasked with the divine assignment of praying for me and giving me permission to unlock all of the greatness inside of me. She discerned that I was trying to carry a load that was too heavy for me to carry alone.

Her very presence and touch, as she gently held me, welcomed me into a safe space that ushered me into the comforting presence of the Lord. There I could be transparent without feeling judged for not knowing, not having faith, and not being confident in my next steps in life. Her presence and love were just what my spirit needed at that moment. After she prayed for me, I knew everything would be OK.

I was graduating. I was not sure how everything was going to work out, but I knew I would be ok. Holy Spirit told me to pack my things I was moving. I went and got some boxes and I started packing. I called my Pastor and told him,

"I am moving!"

He replied, "Oh yeah. Where are you moving to?"

I replied, "I don't know, but God told me, I was moving, so I went and got some boxes and started packing up my things."

Later that week, I received a call from the Director of the ISP stating that she had one spot that had recently become available in the program. If I still wanted it, the spot was mine. I will never forget this day because God showed me, He had truly ordered my steps, and it was the day we lost The King of Pop. Micheal Jackson is a music Icon and legend. I remember the world being so shocked by his sudden death. The air was so electrifying. It was a beautiful day. The sky was so blue and the clouds looked like soft cotton balls. Everywhere you went, you heard fans all around the world paying homage to him by playing his music, while others cried as if they knew him personally. For many of us it felt as if we did. While his family and close friends mourned his death privately, fans did so publicly. We could not believe he was gone.

At first, I was on a natural high, after I found out I got accepted into ISP, this would give me a chance to officially graduate on time, for grad school and provide me with the experience of dorm life due to me spending four to six weeks in Morehouse suites with the other participants in the program. The news losing Micheal made me sober up to the reality of life being fleeting. I was relieved that I got accepted into the ISP, but in the words of King of Blues, B.B. King "The Thrill was gone."

Pearls of Wisdom

Laying On of Hands

- God's dream for you is always bigger than any you can ever imagine, for yourself
- Take limits off that prohibit you from being great.
- Give yourself permission not to always know all the details of your journey of self-discovery.
- Trust the process even when it does not feel good, and you do not know all the details.
- The safest place we can find ourselves is in the presence of God.
- Never underestimate power in the presence of God.
- The laying on of hands has transforming, transferring, therapeutic, and healing capabilities.
- Be careful who you allow yourself to connect with.

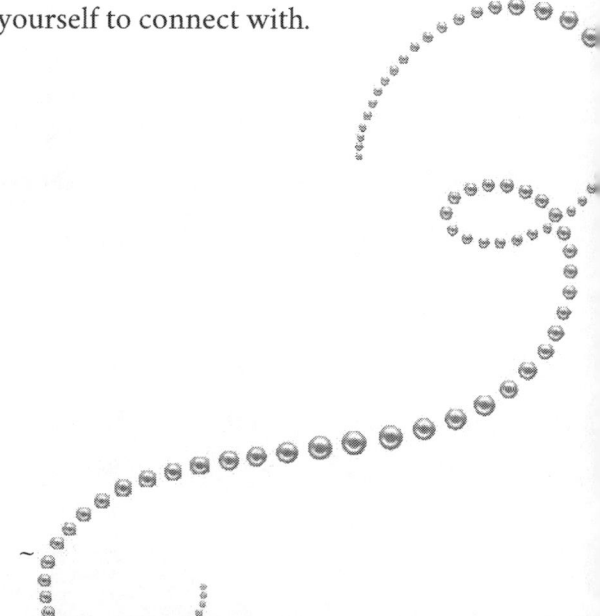

Chapter 20

I Made It

> *Never would have made it. Never could have made it without you. I would have lost it all, but now I see how You were there for me.*
>
> —Marvin Sapp

I made it! I made it, but it was not pretty or easy to achieve my dream of attending Spelman College. To live out your dreams is going to cost you some blood, sweat, tears, time, and sacrifices. There were days I cried out of frustration and irritation. There were days I indulged in throwing myself the best pity party for free $.99.

I made it! I made it, but from a young age, I allowed others to influence me sexually in order to get help with what came easy to others. I held this secret in for years that I was a victim of sexual assault. To this day I still hate the cliché, *What would you do for an A?* I often wonder why we are still measuring people's intellect by the way they regurgitate information and rhetoric. This is clearly an illustration of the banking system of learning. This type of learning style fosters intellectual skills yet it stifles true creativity. Some of the greatest leaders and minds in this world were never great students.

I made it! I made it, but I did not grow up in the best home environment.

The Cosby Show and *A Different World*, gave me hope that I could make it out of the hood through higher education, changing my family legacy, and expanding my social connections.

I made it! I made it, but psychologically I still have to fight within myself against the voice of self-sabotage because of the labels that the education system placed on me. Even though they have been removed, they still challenge me at times, especially in areas related to self-efficacy.

I made it! I made it, but I still hate and struggle with applying for jobs online. There are times when I still feel extremely overwhelmed and not confident in how to sell myself or depict my skill set through writing from an academic lens.

I made it! I made it, but I went to school year-round for four years. It took me four years to earn a two-year degree. My graduation from Spelman has been my favorite graduation thus far. I worked hard for this degree. It cost me something to earn this degree. I was evicted and homeless at one point while I was pursuing this degree. Going to class, I did not fully know how I was going to make it to a friend's house, a friend who allowed me to sleep in her basement. This was a blessing, but she lived so far away, and the bus would not be running by the time I got out of night class.

I made it! I made it, but I lost some loved ones and friends in the pursuit of higher education. My youngest brother was murdered, and I still had to **will** myself to get out of bed every day and go to class. All while bottling up my grief and doing the difficult work to be successful.

I made it! I made it, but it almost killed me. It should not have been this difficult for me to make it. It took me ten years of wandering in the wilderness before I was able to live my dream of attending Spelman College.

I made it! I not only made it, but I am a graduate of Spelman College, class of 2009.

Pearls of Wisdom

I Made It!

- To make it, you must be willing to lose some people and things along the way.
- Never measure your worth by your level of success, accolades, fame, or money.
- Be willing to chase your dream when it looks dead.
- "Fight the good fight of faith" when you feel like you have nothing left to fight with.
- Remember "to whom much is given, much is required."
- Never forget, you were made for this!
- Never forget the shoulders of greatness you stood on to make it.
- Always pay homage and show gratitude.
- Never stay stuck in the success of yesterday. You made it, now what?
- When you make it, remember to hold the door open for the person coming behind.
- Put a price on your worth, but not your integrity.
- Never forget that "The race is not given to the swift, or the strong, but to the one who endures to the end."

Chapter 21

Daring to Dream Beyond Spelman Gates

> *You can't dis or dismiss me. My name is on God's list.*
> *I told you I was made for this!*
>
> —Tanell Vashawn Allen, MDiv

(Original graduate school admission essay, unedited)

My name is Tanell Vashawn Allen, and I am a senior at Spelman College. My major is religious studies. In the past, I have been extremely committed to making the best of my scholastic and extracurricular experiences. I graduated with honors from Elgin Community College in the summer of 2007 and was the commencement speaker for our graduating class. I transferred to Spelman College in the fall of 2007.

I am currently a member of Phi Theta Kappa, the national honor society for two-year colleges, President of Sassy Girl, a club for full-figured women, a volunteer at the Kettle Soup Kitchen, in Elgin, a youth leader, and a member of the evangelist team at Faithwalk Harvest

Center Church. Furthermore, I am a professional hair stylist who has a passion for writing poetry, public speaking, and collecting candles.

I am the first generation of my immediate family to graduate from high school and attend college. I want to set a precedent of higher education for my immediate family. I desire to pass the mantle on to my nephew Lionel, who will graduate from high school in 2010.

My dream since the eleventh grade has been to attend Spelman College. When I got accepted to Spelman, I accomplished a small part of my dream. After I graduate in May 2009, I will have accomplished my goal of graduating from Spelman College.

I have a documented learning disability, but I learned a long time ago never to use my learning disability as a crutch; with hard work, dedication, discipline, and determination, I can achieve any goal and overcome any challenge. When I was in the eighth grade, I had an IEP meeting where a group of educators and the school's psychologist said that I would not graduate from high school; if I did, it would take five years. I graduated in four years from high school, thirteenth in my class with honors, and was a member of the national honor roll society. In my senior year of high school, I had taken the ACT and scored a ten. I was so embarrassed all I could see was failure and defeat. What college would really look at me as a possible student?

I enrolled at Elgin Community College in 2003. Because of the excellent foundation I received at ECC, I knew I had the basic academic skills I needed to be successful at Spelman. It is funny because I always felt in the pit of my stomach that I was put on this earth for a special purpose. My mother taught me a principle that I try to live my life every day: Whatever you do, be the best at it, and do not let anybody tell you or stop you from being the best. Because of that principle, I can say that my distant dream is now about to become a reality.

My major is Religious Studies because I believe my purpose is to inspire through faith. I have a seven-year educational plan that will end with me obtaining doctrines in theology or Christian counseling. I want to empower people for life and not just for the moment, as many athletic coaches do.

When I speak, I feel as if the entire world is sitting still waiting for a profound word to be released to help motivate them to the next level of their destiny. I plan to use my gifts in writing and speaking to restore and encourage others that they can reach their full potential.

I plan to use my knowledge of diverse systems of faith to be a motivational speaker and preacher. My goal as a speaker is to empower people-based faith, hard work, and the three D's of success that I previously mentioned.

I want to inspire and challenge others to aspire for more in life. As a religious studies student, I am taught to think outside of the box of what is deemed normal. By thinking outside of the box, I have learned why people are so passionate about what they believe in.

I simply want to remind people that they have a purpose and a plan that was predestined for their lives. It is impossible to convince them of this if I do not know anything about their diverse religious backgrounds. Also studying religion from an academic lens adds a different perspective.

In addition to it breaking some of the stereotypes I had about other faith systems that I was socialized to believe due to a lack of knowledge and understanding of different religions. My major will make me a more diverse speaker in the public speaking and preaching arenas as well.

After I graduate from Spelman College in 2009, I plan to attend Harvard University, Howard, Emory, or Georgia State for graduate school. I am not sure which graduate school I will attend. However, I plan to work for Teach for America while I am in graduate school. I plan to get into a Masters of Divinity program that will build upon my Bachelor of Arts degree in the field of religious studies.

After graduate school, I want to get my doctrines in Christian counseling. To obtain a doctrine in Christian Counseling would be a vast need met in the Christian community. I think that it would be more than beneficial to me as an empowerment coach. I would have the knowledge and understanding to counsel people spiritually and mentally.

End of Chapter Discussion Questions

I Am Not Stupid, Dumb, or Crazy

1. Do you think Oprah Winfrey will let the author teach one of her Master Life Classes?
2. Why or why not?

Trading Touches for Help

1. Do you think the author's need to please her teacher and be deemed smart led her to trade touches for help?
2. Do you think the older student took advantage of her?
3. Why or why not?

My Baby Leaped

1. Has there ever been a time in your life that you felt like your baby, or purpose leaped?
2. If so, what caused it to leap?

I Am a Dreamer

1. Why do you think the author fought so hard for her dream to attend Spelman College?
2. Why do you think the two words "I am" held so much power for the author?

Crying in the Closet

1. Do you think the author was used to suffering alone emotionally and mentally due to her having a learning disability?

2. Do you think the author was having a meltdown because she procrastinated as opposed to having a learning disability?

3. What is one thing you have learned about yourself due to procrastination?

Tearing Down My Rocky Foundation

1. Do you think Dr. Black was too hard on the author?

2. Do you agree that the author's academic foundation was rocky?

3. Why do you think the author asked Dr. Black to write her a letter of recommendation?

I Am Your Pusher

1. Do you think the author still would have made it to Spelman College without her Pushers?

2. Who are your Pushers in your life?

3. Do you think Pushers are important?

4. Why or why not?

The Hardest Thing

1. Do you think the author was wrong for not taking time to fully grieve the loss of her brother?

2. Why or why?

3. What is the hardest thing you have had to deal with while trying to achieve your dream?

My Math is Bad Two Years Equals Four Years

1. Why do you think it took the author so long to graduate from Elgin Community College?
2. Do you think it took her a long time because of her own actions?
3. Why or not?

Taking Off the Labels

1. Do you think labels hold power over us?
2. Do you think the author was able to flip the label and make it work for her, or was she able to take it off?
3. Why, or why not?
4. Do you think the author's grandmother Foxy believed in the label that was placed on her?

Kicking Down Doors

1. Do you think people should kick down doors that they were denied access to, or create their own?
2. Which would you prefer to do?
3. How did the author kick down the door to attend Spelman College?

Not Everybody Is Going to Be Happy for You

1. Do you think the author's mother was telling the truth when she told her "Everybody is not going to be happy for you!"
2. Why do you think the author's mother was so hard on her?
3. Can you recall a time in your life when it seemed like someone did not celebrate your success with you?

4. How did you handle it?

"Can You Wear White Young Lady?"

1. Do you think the author's mother meant to tell her to settle for a white skirt and white shirt?
2. Why or why not?
3. What do you think of Spelman College's use of full-body Polaroid pictures?
4. Do you think Spelman College requiring a full-body polaroid is true, or is this another stereotype about Spelman College?
5. Why or why not.

Living the Dream

1. Do you think the author was really living her dream or the dream God had for her?
2. Why or why not?
3. Where do you think most dreams and ambitions come from?
4. What is a current dream you are aspiring to achieve?

Faith Laced with Grief and Depression

1. Do you think it is possible to be a person of faith and suffer from depression?
2. Why or why not?
3. Do you think people can use their faith as a coping mechanism to deal with stress and depression?
4. If so, how can they use it?

"Harpo Who That Man Is?"

1. What do you think was the first red flag about Winston?

2. Do you think the author should have stayed in a relationship with Win, after finding out about his double life?

3. Would you have stood by your partner's side if they were charged with rape or another serious crime?

4. Do you think the ladies in the cafeteria were wrong for gossiping about the author?

History in the Making

1. Do you think the author should have voted for Barack Obama because they both are African American, regardless of his credentials or political party?

2. Do you think the author really understood her role as a voter?

3. What are your thoughts about America electing its first Black president?

4. How did this make you feel?

5. Can you think of any historical moments in your life that made you feel like you were witnessing history in the making?

6. Do you think the fears that some older African Americans had were valid?

7. Can you name something you feel led to do, but are afraid of doing, and why?

8. Why do you think we should still do things that we are afraid of doing?

9. If you could make your mark on history, how and what would you do?

When Man Says No, but God Says Yes

1. Why do you think the author was determined to take Spanish classes even when there was a loophole to exempt her from taking them?
2. Do you think the author should have taken the loophole?
3. Why or why not?
4. Do you think the program director was slightly biased towards the author?
5. Why or why not?
6. Is there something man has said No to you about in your life, but God has said Yes?

Laying On of Hands

1. Why do you think the author was anxious about the next steps in her life after graduating from Spelman College?
2. Have you ever been anxious about the next steps in your life?
3. Why or why not?
4. What did you do to help you get through it?
5. Do you think every college should have a Laying On of Hands to affirm its graduates?
6. Why do you think the author experienced so much peace after this service?
7. Do you think the Intensive Spanish Program (ISP) gave the author the college dorm life she longed to experience?
8. Why or why not?

9. Do you remember the icon who died on the day that the author was accepted into the (ISP)?

10. Where were you and how did you feel?

I Made It!

1. Why do you think the author reiterated so many times that she made it?

2. What is the hardest thing you think the author had to overcome to make it?

3. What are some things you need to overcome to make it?

4. How will you work on your goals to do so?

Made in the USA
Columbia, SC
19 August 2024

6c420d72-e25a-4c1e-9aeb-04b538456e0aR01